MARY
QUEEN OF SCOTS

MARY
QUEEN OF SCOTS

Sally Stepanek

CHELSEA HOUSE PUBLISHERS
NEW YORK
PHILADELPHIA

EDITORIAL DIRECTOR: Nancy Toff
MANAGING EDITOR: Karyn Gullen Browne
COPY CHIEF: Perry Scott King
ART DIRECTOR: Giannella Garrett
PICTURE EDITOR: Elizabeth Terhune

Staff for MARY, QUEEN OF SCOTS

SENIOR EDITOR: John W. Selfridge
ASSISTANT EDITORS: Maria Behan, Pierre Hauser, Bert Yaeger
COPY EDITORS: Sean Dolan, Kathleen McDermott
ASSISTANT DESIGNER: Noreen Lamb
PICTURE RESEARCH: Ian Ensign
LAYOUT: David Murray
PRODUCTION COORDINATOR: Alma Rodriguez
PRODUCTION ASSISTANT: Karen Dreste
COVER DESIGN: Robin Peterson

CREATIVE DIRECTOR: Harold Steinberg

3 5 7 9 8 6 4

Frontispiece: portrait of Mary, Queen of Scots by François Clouet

Library of Congress Cataloging in Publication Data

Stepanek, Sally. MARY, QUEEN OF SCOTS

(World leaders past & present)
Bibliography: p.
Includes index.
1. Mary, Queen of Scots, 1542–1587. 2. Scotland—Kings
and rulers—Biography— Juvenile literature. 3. Scotland—
History—Mary Stuart, 1542–1587— Juvenile literature.
[1. Mary, Queen of Scots, 1542–1587. 2. Kings, queens,
rulers, etc. 3. Scotland—History—Mary Stuart, 1542–1587]
I. Title. II. Series.
DA787.A1S87 1986   941.105′092′4 [B] [92]   86—20709

ISBN 0-87754-540-5
    0-7910-0655-7 (PBK)

Contents

JOHN ADAMS
JOHN QUINCY ADAMS
KONRAD ADENAUER
ALEXANDER THE GREAT
SALVADOR ALLENDE
MARC ANTONY
CORAZON AQUINO
YASIR ARAFAT
KING ARTHUR
HAFEZ AL-ASSAD
KEMAL ATATÜRK
ATTILA
CLEMENT ATTLEE
AUGUSTUS CAESAR
MENACHEM BEGIN
DAVID BEN-GURION
OTTO VON BISMARCK
LÉON BLUM
SIMON BOLÍVAR
CESARE BORGIA
WILLY BRANDT
LEONID BREZHNEV
JULIUS CAESAR
JOHN CALVIN
JIMMY CARTER
FIDEL CASTRO
CATHERINE THE GREAT
CHARLEMAGNE
CHIANG KAI-SHEK
WINSTON CHURCHILL
GEORGES CLEMENCEAU
CLEOPATRA
CONSTANTINE THE GREAT
HERNÁN CORTÉS
OLIVER CROMWELL
GEORGES-JACQUES
    DANTON
JEFFERSON DAVIS
MOSHE DAYAN
CHARLES DE GAULLE
EAMON DE VALERA
EUGENE DEBS
DENG XIAOPING
BENJAMIN DISRAELI
ALEXANDER DUBČEK
FRANÇOIS & JEAN-CLAUDE
    DUVALIER
DWIGHT EISENHOWER
ELEANOR OF AQUITAINE
ELIZABETH I
FAISAL
FERDINAND & ISABELLA
FRANCISCO FRANCO
BENJAMIN FRANKLIN

FREDERICK THE GREAT
INDIRA GANDHI
MOHANDAS GANDHI
GIUSEPPE GARIBALDI
AMIN & BASHIR GEMAYEL
GENGHIS KHAN
WILLIAM GLADSTONE
MIKHAIL GORBACHEV
ULYSSES S. GRANT
ERNESTO "CHE" GUEVARA
TENZIN GYATSO
ALEXANDER HAMILTON
DAG HAMMARSKJÖLD
HENRY VIII
HENRY OF NAVARRE
PAUL VON HINDENBURG
HIROHITO
ADOLF HITLER
HO CHI MINH
KING HUSSEIN
IVAN THE TERRIBLE
ANDREW JACKSON
JAMES I
WOJCIECH JARUZELSKI
THOMAS JEFFERSON
JOAN OF ARC
POPE JOHN XXIII
POPE JOHN PAUL II
LYNDON JOHNSON
BENITO JUÁREZ
JOHN KENNEDY
ROBERT KENNEDY
JOMO KENYATTA
AYATOLLAH KHOMEINI
NIKITA KHRUSHCHEV
KIM IL SUNG
MARTIN LUTHER KING, JR.
HENRY KISSINGER
KUBLAI KHAN
LAFAYETTE
ROBERT E. LEE
VLADIMIR LENIN
ABRAHAM LINCOLN
DAVID LLOYD GEORGE
LOUIS XIV
MARTIN LUTHER
JUDAS MACCABEUS
JAMES MADISON
NELSON & WINNIE
    MANDELA
MAO ZEDONG
FERDINAND MARCOS
GEORGE MARSHALL

MARY, QUEEN OF SCOTS
TOMÁŠ MASARYK
GOLDA MEIR
KLEMENS VON METTERNICH
JAMES MONROE
HOSNI MUBARAK
ROBERT MUGABE
BENITO MUSSOLINI
NAPOLÉON BONAPARTE
GAMAL ABDEL NASSER
JAWAHARLAL NEHRU
NERO
NICHOLAS II
RICHARD NIXON
KWAME NKRUMAH
DANIEL ORTEGA
MOHAMMED REZA PAHLAVI
THOMAS PAINE
CHARLES STEWART
    PARNELL
PERICLES
JUAN PERÓN
PETER THE GREAT
POL POT
MUAMMAR EL-QADDAFI
RONALD REAGAN
CARDINAL RICHELIEU
MAXIMILIEN ROBESPIERRE
ELEANOR ROOSEVELT
FRANKLIN ROOSEVELT
THEODORE ROOSEVELT
ANWAR SADAT
HAILE SELASSIE
PRINCE SIHANOUK
JAN SMUTS
JOSEPH STALIN
SUKARNO
SUN YAT-SEN
TAMERLANE
MOTHER TERESA
MARGARET THATCHER
JOSIP BROZ TITO
TOUSSAINT L'OUVERTURE
LEON TROTSKY
PIERRE TRUDEAU
HARRY TRUMAN
QUEEN VICTORIA
LECH WALESA
GEORGE WASHINGTON
CHAIM WEIZMANN
WOODROW WILSON
XERXES
EMILIANO ZAPATA
ZHOU ENLAI

CHELSEA HOUSE PUBLISHERS

ON LEADERSHIP
Arthur M. Schlesinger, jr.

LEADERSHIP, it may be said, is really what makes the world go round. Love no doubt smooths the passage; but love is a private transaction between consenting adults. Leadership is a public transaction with history. The idea of leadership affirms the capacity of individuals to move, inspire, and mobilize masses of people so that they act together in pursuit of an end. Sometimes leadership serves good purposes, sometimes bad; but whether the end is benign or evil, great leaders are those men and women who leave their personal stamp on history.

Now, the very concept of leadership implies the proposition that individuals can make a difference. This proposition has never been universally accepted. From classical times to the present day, eminent thinkers have regarded individuals as no more than the agents and pawns of larger forces, whether the gods and goddesses of the ancient world or, in the modern era, race, class, nation, the dialectic, the will of the people, the spirit of the times, history itself. Against such forces, the individual dwindles into insignificance.

So contends the thesis of historical determinism. Tolstoy's great novel *War and Peace* offers a famous statement of the case. Why, Tolstoy asked, did millions of men in the Napoleonic wars, denying their human feelings and their common sense, move back and forth across Europe slaughtering their fellows? "The war," Tolstoy answered, "was bound to happen simply because it was bound to happen." All prior history predetermined it. As for leaders, they, Tolstoy said, "are but the labels that serve to give a name to an end and, like labels, they have the least possible connection with the event." The greater the leader, "the more conspicuous the inevitability and the predestination of every act he commits." The leader, said Tolstoy, is "the slave of history."

Determinism takes many forms. Marxism is the determinism of class. Nazism the determinism of race. But the idea of men and women as the slaves of history runs athwart the deepest human instincts. Rigid determinism abolishes the idea of human freedom—

the assumption of free choice that underlies every move we make, every word we speak, every thought we think. It abolishes the idea of human responsibility, since it is manifestly unfair to reward or punish people for actions that are by definition beyond their control. No one can live consistently by any deterministic creed. The Marxist states prove this themselves by their extreme susceptibility to the cult of leadership.

More than that, history refutes the idea that individuals make no difference. In December 1931 a British politician crossing Park Avenue in New York City between 76th and 77th Streets around 10:30 P.M. looked in the wrong direction and was knocked down by an automobile—a moment, he later recalled, of a man aghast, a world aglare: "I do not understand why I was not broken like an eggshell or squashed like a gooseberry." Fourteen months later an American politician, sitting in an open car in Miami, Florida, was fired on by an assassin; the man beside him was hit. Those who believe that individuals make no difference to history might well ponder whether the next two decades would have been the same had Mario Constasino's car killed Winston Churchill in 1931 and Giuseppe Zangara's bullet killed Franklin Roosevelt in 1933. Suppose, in addition, that Adolf Hitler had been killed in the street fighting during the Munich *Putsch* of 1923 and that Lenin had died of typhus during World War I. What would the 20th century be like now?

For better or for worse, individuals do make a difference. "The notion that a people can run itself and its affairs anonymously," wrote the philosopher William James, "is now well known to be the silliest of absurdities. Mankind does nothing save through initiatives on the part of inventors, great or small, and imitation by the rest of us—these are the sole factors in human progress. Individuals of genius show the way, and set the patterns, which common people then adopt and follow."

Leadership, James suggests, means leadership in thought as well as in action. In the long run, leaders in thought may well make the greater difference to the world. But, as Woodrow Wilson once said, "Those only are leaders of men, in the general eye, who lead in action. . . . It is at their hands that new thought gets its translation into the crude language of deeds." Leaders in thought often invent in solitude and obscurity, leaving to later generations the tasks of imitation. Leaders in action—the leaders portrayed in this series—have to be effective in their own time.

And they cannot be effective by themselves. They must act in response to the rhythms of their age. Their genius must be adapted, in a phrase of William James's, "to the receptivities of the moment." Leaders are useless without followers. "There goes the mob," said the French politician hearing a clamor in the streets. "I am their leader. I must follow them." Great leaders turn the inchoate emotions of the mob to purposes of their own. They seize on the opportunities of their time, the hopes, fears, frustrations, crises, potentialities. They succeed when events have prepared the way for them, when the community is awaiting to be aroused, when they can provide the clarifying and organizing ideas. Leadership ignites the circuit between the individual and the mass and thereby alters history.

It may alter history for better or for worse. Leaders have been responsible for the most extravagant follies and most monstrous crimes that have beset suffering humanity. They have also been vital in such gains as humanity has made in individual freedom, religious and racial tolerance, social justice and respect for human rights.

There is no sure way to tell in advance who is going to lead for good and who for evil. But a glance at the gallery of men and women in *World Leaders—Past and Present* suggests some useful tests.

One test is this: do leaders lead by force or by persuasion? By command or by consent? Through most of history leadership was exercised by the divine right of authority. The duty of followers was to defer and to obey. "Theirs not to reason why,/ Theirs but to do and die." On occasion, as with the so-called "enlightened despots" of the 18th century in Europe, absolutist leadership was animated by humane purposes. More often, absolutism nourished the passion for domination, land, gold and conquest and resulted in tyranny.

The great revolution of modern times has been the revolution of equality. The idea that all people should be equal in their legal condition has undermined the old structure of authority, hierarchy and deference. The revolution of equality has had two contrary effects on the nature of leadership. For equality, as Alexis de Tocqueville pointed out in his great study *Democracy in America*, might mean equality in servitude as well as equality in freedom.

"I know of only two methods of establishing equality in the political world," Tocqueville wrote. "Rights must be given to every citizen, or none at all to anyone . . . save one, who is the master of all." There was no middle ground "between the sovereignty of all and the absolute power of one man." In his astonishing prediction of 20th-century totalitarian dictatorship, Tocqueville explained how the revolution of equality could lead to the *"Führerprinzip"* and more terrible absolutism than the world had ever known.

But when rights are given to every citizen and the sovereignty of all is established, the problem of leadership takes a new form, becomes more exacting than ever before. It is easy to issue commands and enforce them by the rope and the stake, the concentration camp and the *gulag.* It is much harder to use argument and achievement to overcome opposition and win consent. The Founding Fathers of the United States understood the difficulty. They believed that history had given them the opportunity to decide, as Alexander Hamilton wrote in the first Federalist Paper, whether men are indeed capable of basing government on "reflection and choice, or whether they are forever destined to depend . . . on accident and force."

Government by reflection and choice called for a new style of leadership and a new quality of followership. It required leaders to be responsive to popular concerns, and it required followers to be active and informed participants in the process. Democracy does not eliminate emotion from politics; sometimes it fosters demagoguery; but it is confident that, as the greatest of democratic leaders put it, you cannot fool all of the people all of the time. It measures leadership by results and retires those who overreach or falter or fail.

It is true that in the long run despots are measured by results too. But they can postpone the day of judgment, sometimes indefinitely, and in the meantime they can do infinite harm. It is also true that democracy is no guarantee of virtue and intelligence in government, for the voice of the people is not necessarily the voice of God. But democracy, by assuring the right of opposition, offers built-in resistance to the evils inherent in absolutism. As the theologian Reinhold Niebuhr summed it up, "Man's capacity for justice makes democracy possible, but man's inclination to injustice makes democracy necessary."

A second test for leadership is the end for which power is sought. When leaders have as their goal the supremacy of a master race or the promotion of totalitarian revolution or the acquisition and exploitation of colonies or the protection of greed and privilege or the preservation of personal power, it is likely that their leadership will do little to advance the cause of humanity. When their goal is the abolition of slavery, the liberation of women, the enlargement of opportunity for the poor and powerless, the extension of equal rights to racial minorities, the defense of the freedoms of expression and opposition, it is likely that their leadership will increase the sum of human liberty and welfare.

Leaders have done great harm to the world. They have also conferred great benefits. You will find both sorts in this series. Even "good" leaders must be regarded with a certain wariness. Leaders are not demigods; they put on their trousers one leg after another just like ordinary mortals. No leader is infallible, and every leader needs to be reminded of this at regular intervals. Irreverence irritates leaders but is their salvation. Unquestioning submission corrupts leaders and demands followers. Making a cult of a leader is always a mistake. Fortunately hero worship generates its own antidote. "Every hero," said Emerson, "becomes a bore at last."

The signal benefit the great leaders confer is to embolden the rest of us to live according to our own best selves, to be active, insistent, and resolute in affirming our own sense of things. For great leaders attest to the reality of human freedom against the supposed inevitabilities of history. And they attest to the wisdom and power that may lie within the most unlikely of us, which is why Abraham Lincoln remains the supreme example of great leadership. A great leader, said Emerson, exhibits new possibilities to all humanity. "We feed on genius. . . . Great men exist that there may be greater men."

Great leaders, in short, justify themselves by emancipating and empowering their followers. So humanity struggles to master its destiny, remembering with Alexis de Tocqueville: "It is true that around every man a fatal circle is traced beyond which he cannot pass; but within the wide verge of that circle he is powerful and free; as it is with man, so with communities."

1
The Trial in the Tower

The old woman hardly heard the evening drumroll below her prison tower. As she sat alone in a halo of candlelight, her twisted hands worked a gold needle and thread through a miniature tapestry with a dexterity born of long hours of labor. A panorama of embroidered ships and castles covered the walls around her. Indeed, by 1586 the woman had been working for many years.

Suddenly, the prison door opened and an armed messenger stepped inside, paused, and then proclaimed, in clear words that echoed through the barren cell, "You shall be tried for high treason on the morrow!" With dignity the prisoner stood slowly, adjusted the heavy crucifix about her neck, gave her needlework to the messenger, and said, "A present for my dear cousin and captor, Queen Elizabeth!"

In the shadows, the man tried with some difficulty to make out the image on the "gift" — a ghostly hawk, in whose talons hung a cowering bird in a cage. Once he divined the picture's meaning, he threw the tapestry to the floor and said angrily, "Tomorrow morning at nine o'clock — prepare to hear your death sentence!" Leaving the cell, he turned the gate key with a flourish and the captive was alone once more, left to contemplate her fate in silence and darkness.

> *Even in the eyes of her enemies, her Catholicism came to outweigh her moral shortcomings as her chief crime.*
> —IAN B. COWAN
> Scottish historian

Mary Stuart swears to her English inquisitors in 1586 that she has not conspired to assassinate Queen Elizabeth I. Mary and Elizabeth, though cousins, were bitter rivals for power as the monarchs of Scotland and England and also as representatives of their competing religions, Catholicism and Protestantism.

In 1586 Mary (seated, top right) was tried for treason by an English council at Fotheringhay Castle. She had been accused of plotting with a Catholic conspirator, Anthony Babington, and an English Jesuit priest to seize the throne from Elizabeth. Sir Francis Walsingham, Elizabeth's private secretary, had uncovered the scheme by reading Mary's prison correspondence.

The Roman church, once the holiest of all, has become the most licentious den of thieves, the most shameless of all brothels, the kingdom of sin, death, and hell.

—MARTIN LUTHER
father of the
Protestant Reformation

The following morning, the prisoner was escorted from her tower in Fotheringhay Castle. Sadly, she could hardly make her way without the help of attendants; two decades of captivity had dimmed her eyesight and bowed her spine. Her clothes, too, were tattered, their colors faded. At 44 years old, she looked like a woman at the end of her life. Nonetheless, she carried herself with full regal majesty, for this was Mary Stuart, queen of the Scots.

The queen's days of court masques and hunts were long gone. By the time of her appearance in court, Mary had outlasted three husbands and she had not seen her only son in more than 19 years. She had lost many friends and lovers, and had gained even more enemies. She had lost her Scottish kingdom, and was on the brink of losing her life.

As the Scottish queen walked past the 40 English earls, justices, barons, and councilors who had gathered for the trial, they shouted, "Whore!" "Murderess!" "Traitor!" Mary proudly lifted her velvet gown and took her place in the prisoner's chair. She was ready to hear the charges against her that had been drawn up by the highest councils of the English queen, Elizabeth I.

As the court came to order, the earl of Kent called out in a rumbling voice that shook Mary to the bone, "Your death, Madam, is the life of our religion, as your life would be its death!" Mary was not fooled by this trial for treason, adultery, and murder. Her real predicament was known to all present: Mary was caught in the religious war between Catholics and Protestants, a war which had been raging in Europe since the beginning of the 16th century. As a Catholic in the gathering storm, Mary was at a decided disadvantage in a court of law in Protestant England. In a lifetime of constant battle, this confrontation with the queen was to be Mary's last.

The kingdom of Scotland had been a Catholic nation united under the rule of the pope for almost 500 years. With the teachings of Martin Luther, a German monk who preached and wrote in the first half of the 16th century, the religious traditions of the Catholic church were called into question. In fact, Luther's challenge was so provocative that he was responsible for setting into motion a religious revolution called the Protestant Reformation.

When Luther examined the Catholic church in Germany and Italy, he saw empty rituals, ignorant and profiteering clergy, and false doctrines. Luther was especially outraged by the Church's sale of "indulgences," which were "heavenly certificates" guaranteeing the forgiveness of sins.

On October 31, 1517, Luther posted 95 complaints, or "theses," on the door of the castle church of Wittenberg. His general message was forthright and accessible; his motto was a verse from Romans in the New Testament: "The just shall live by faith." Christians, Luther preached, did not need the hierarchy of priest, bishop, and pope, or the Catholic

Standing before the door of the castle church at Wittenberg, Germany, in October 1517, Martin Luther posts his 95 "complaints" against the Catholic church. Luther preached that individual faith, not the Church, would assure salvation, a concept that sparked the Protestant Reformation in Europe. England, adopting the new religion, soon broke from the papal authority in Rome, but the Stuart royal family of Scotland remained Catholic.

King James V of Scotland, from a carving on the wall of Stirling Castle. James died in 1542 shortly after failing in a religious crusade against England; he never saw his baby daughter, Mary. At the age of one week, the infant became queen of the Scots.

traditions of prayers and sacrifices. "If a Christian has faith," proclaimed Luther, "he has everything." Soon his ideas were copied by oppressed Germans and turned into something of an anti-Catholic manifesto. His teachings spread through continental Europe and to Scotland and England as well. Yet the Scottish Catholics disagreed: they stuck to their belief that the pope was the head of the Church and that the Church was necessary for salvation.

At the time, the Catholic church was extremely wealthy and politically very powerful. As the most powerful religious figure in western Europe, the pope was able to form strong alliances with many European emperors and princes. Thus, the new Protestant teachings posed a considerable threat to the political balance of church and state. Some rulers broke away from the Church's rule and created their own Protestant sect, such as Henry VIII and the Anglican church of England. Others, such as Henry II of France and James V of Scotland, remained loyal to the pope. As tensions increased, the Protestants established many "free churches" throughout Europe.

By the early 1520s, Luther's writings began to spread among the Scottish, causing great division in the government and populace. In 1525 Scotland's Parliament condemned all Protestant literature coming into the country. In November 1542 King James V of Scotland, who reigned from 1513 to 1542, a faithful Catholic who would not tolerate the new Protestant teachings, led a crusade, or religious war, against England. The Scots, however, suffered a terrible defeat in the Battle of Solway Moss, where 1,200 men were taken captive. Such were the extremes of feeling and action that had come to characterize the Reformation movement and reaction to it.

One month after James's defeat, he lay dying — some say of a broken spirit — in the Scottish city of Falkland. Into this turmoil and unrest, Mary Stuart was born. One week later, King James V died, passing the crown into the young infant's hands.

Mary inherited a land only beginning to feel the tremors of religious conflict. Hers would be a difficult reign of transition: her father's kingdom had been Catholic while her own rule would be a labor of constant struggles as the Scottish nation suffered the birth pangs of the new Protestant religion. Caught between two faiths, Mary would be scorned by both sides and forced to rely on her own political judgment — which many historians say was sorely lacking. As perhaps one of the most colorful queens in history, the life of Mary Stuart is still shrouded in mystery.

> *All men lamented that the realm was left without a male to succeed.*
> —JOHN KNOX leader of the Scottish Protestants, on the death of King James V and Mary's inheritance of the throne

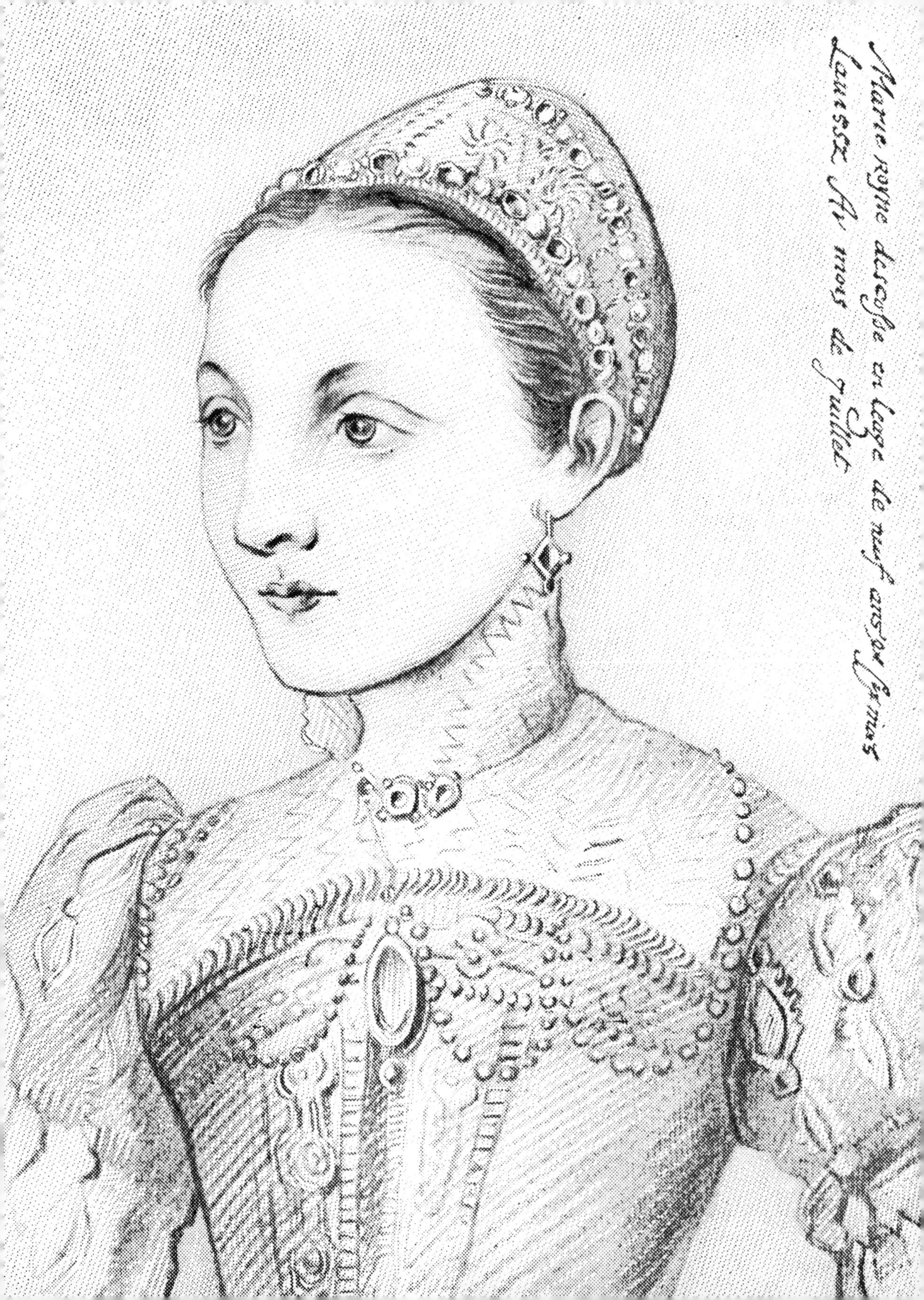

2

Battles for an Infant Queen

December 8, 1542, was a day of rejoicing at Lin-lithgow Palace. The royal residence, surrounded by a peaceful lake, dominated West Lothian, 16 miles from the Scottish capital of Edinburgh. This was lowland country: the fields had few trees or bushes, icy marshes and lakes spotted the landscape, and sheep in heavy winter fleece roamed peacefully on the hills.

The banqueting tables of Linlithgow were spread for a feast. Salted mutton and geese, as well as sweet, imported cakes and pastries were just some of the delicacies laid out for the assembled family and friends. Minstrels and jesters danced around the fountain in the interior courtyard. Peasants crowded near the palace's outer drawbridge, hoping to catch a glimpse of the royal celebration. A new princess — a rightful heir to the Scottish throne — had been born.

One year earlier, the king and queen's two infant sons had died, leaving the royal couple without a successor. Although King James had at least seven

Sundry parts of this realm, which has been ever Catholic since the beginning of the faith to these days, are now infected with the pestilent heresies of Luther.
—section of Scottish bishops' proclamation, 1547

This crayon drawing of Mary at age nine was commissioned by Catherine de Médicis, wife of King Henry II of France. At her birth in 1542 Mary became a pawn in the struggle for control over her country that was being waged not only by Catholics and Protestants but also by the English, Spanish, and French royal families.

Robert I, the Bruce, who was king of Scotland from 1306 to 1329. He was a mighty warrior as well; at the Battle of Bannockburn in 1314, he led his greatly outnumbered troops to victory over the English. Through his daughter, Marjory, the Stuarts became the royal family of Scotland.

illegitimate children, none were considered eligible for the crown. According to the laws of Scottish inheritance, the right to the throne had to be passed by direct descent through the rightful queen, in this case, Marie de Guise. With the birth of Mary Stuart, the court had reason to rejoice: the crown would remain in the family.

King James lay dying at Falkland when news came from Linlithgow of his daughter's birth. "The devil go with it!" he exclaimed in dismay. "It came with a lass, it will pass with a lass!" James had little confidence in the power of a woman sovereign. Although the crown came to the Stuarts through a woman — Marjory, the daughter of Robert the Bruce, who had ruled Scotland from 1306 to 1329 — James prophesied that the family would lose its power through the weakness of his daughter. James died just days after this dour pronouncement, and the one-week-old Mary became the queen of Scotland.

The birth and death came at a critical time in Scottish history. James's passing left the country weak and leaderless. Two parties quickly confronted each other in a battle for power: the Catholics, led by the queen mother, Marie de Guise, and the most powerful man in the Catholic church, the wealthy and clever Cardinal David Beaton; against the Protestants, led by the second earl of Arran, James Hamilton. Because he had the support of an increasingly vocal pro-English minority and was a descendant of King James II and an heir to the throne if Mary died, the earl was proclaimed regent, or "governor of the realm," on January 3, 1543. This meant that he was to rule until Mary came of age in her 12th year. However, this Protestant regent was not widely supported since the majority of the Scottish were still Catholic and still recognized the primacy of papal power.

Meanwhile, the English king, Henry VIII, was planning to overtake divided Scotland — and it appeared to him that Arran might be a valuable ally. Ultimately, though, Henry realized that he needed more than a weak regent to unite the two countries, and so he took another route. Since politically mo-

The Tower of London was long one of the most famous prisons in the world. In 1542 Henry VIII jailed 1,200 Catholic Scotsmen there after defeating James V in the Battle of Solway Moss. He released them as part of his cunning attempt to secure the infant Mary as a bride for his son and so unite England and Scotland.

tivated royal marriages were a common practice of the time, Henry, thinking that such a union would secure an alliance between Scotland and England, began to press for a wedding between his five-year-old son and heir, Prince Edward (by his wife Jane Seymour), and the infant Queen Mary. To persuade the wary Scots, Henry ordered the release of the 1,200 prisoners he had kept in the Tower of London since the Battle of Solway Moss. Upon their release, the Scottish lords signed an article persuading the earl of Arran to agree to the marriage. Henry's plan was under way.

Both Cardinal Beaton and Marie de Guise were vehemently opposed to the marriage. In July 1543 Beaton and some of his associates took the infant queen and her mother to Stirling Castle, the strongest fortress in Scotland. There, high upon a rock above Bannockburn, Mary was safe from the designs of the earl and Henry VIII. In September Beaton had Mary officially crowned as queen in a small, solemn ceremony aimed at assuring the Scots that the real power rested in Catholic hands — the hands of Mary Stuart.

But the cardinal was powerless to stop the governing lords of Scotland. By the Treaties of Greenwich, signed on July 1, 1543, and ratified by the regent in Edinburgh in August, the Scottish Parliament promised Mary to the English prince upon her 11th birthday. The treaty was quite unpopular with the Scots, especially considering Henry's suspicious attempts to change the terms of the agreement so that he could gain actual possession of the baby several years before the marriage. The Catholics also opposed Henry's demand that Scotland break their traditional alliance with the Catholic nation of France.

THE BETTMANN ARCHIVE

King Henry VIII ruled England from 1509 until his death in 1547. He remained Catholic until the Church forbade him to divorce his wife, Catherine of Aragon, who had not given birth to the male heir he so badly wanted. In response, Henry founded the Protestant Church of England, of which he, as king, would be head.

Fearing a mass uprising, at the end of the year the Scottish government reneged on its promise of marriage. The English revenge was swift and ambitious. On an early May morning in 1544, English ships were seen in the Firth of Forth, a river inlet extending from the North Sea to Edinburgh; the English earl of Hertford and his army had arrived, apparently hoping to capture the capital and kidnap the young queen. As the English standards loomed perilously close to the Scottish capital, Marie de Guise secreted her young daughter in the hidden chambers of Stirling Castle.

The ensuing war of "rough wooing" — so named for Henry's violent efforts to win over the Scots — lasted for two years. The French came to the aid of the weakening Scots, but soon all of southern Scotland smoldered with the fires of Hertford's army, which had been instructed to inflict maximum damage. Both Beaton and the earl of Arran, discredited by their failed leadership, fled to Linlithgow Palace; although the English were strong, they were not able to take this important castle. Scotland was devastated, but Queen Mary was still at Stirling Castle, safe and sound.

Though Cardinal Beaton had died in 1546 and Henry VIII in 1547, the earl of Hertford continued the war by attacking Scotland a second time. At the Battle of Pinkie near Edinburgh, in September 1547, the Scots were again defeated in the bloodiest war they had seen, with thousands slain and 1,500 prisoners taken. The Scottish still refer to this battle

Stirling Castle, the Scottish stronghold where the infant Queen Mary was taken in 1543. Mary was hidden there to protect her from Henry's political ploys and from English troops during the war of "rough wooing," which ensued when the Scots refused to accept the marriage alliance with England. Both Mary and her son, James VI, would be crowned here.

as "Black Saturday." But even though they inflicted enormous casualties on their enemy, the English were unable to seize the young Queen Mary.

Adding to the general hostility was England's resentment of Scotland's alliance with the French, who came to their aid in the various wars. Despite threats from England, France stood by its commitment to help the crippled country. In addition, the French king, Henry II, offered to guard Mary in his court and raise her with all the splendor of a French princess in the court of Valois. Marie de Guise was overjoyed at this prospect. Marie had been a French princess before becoming queen of Scotland, and still had deep allegiances to her native land.

France's efforts were, however, far from altruistic; like the English, the French also hoped to control Scotland. When it was decided to give Mary to the French, Henry II did not mask his plans for Mary's kingdom. Having barely escaped the prison of one royal marriage, Mary was about to find herself being prepared for another. Barely old enough to walk, Mary was perhaps the most coveted bride in all of Europe, a bride of convenience, not of love.

At the Battle of Pinkie in 1547, Scottish and English troops engaged in one of the fiercest encounters the country had ever seen. After this bloody defeat the Scots decided to accept the offer of King Henry II of France to raise Mary in his court, where she would be safe from the English.

3

The Prisms of the Crown

In late July 1548 Mary's mother stood high atop Dumbarton Rock, overlooking the Clyde River, shielding herself against a fierce thunderstorm. Through the rain she could hardly distinguish the distant French ship from the high, gray seas. The royal galley was sailing to Roscoff, France, with her child queen.

For days the ship had lain at anchor, waiting for the weather to clear. Finally the vessel set sail, making its way south around the Isle of Man, Wales, and the West Country before reaching the English Channel. Mary was sailing for her new French home, where her life, hoped Marie de Guise, would be much less stormy than the seas she had to cross to get there.

Earlier that month, a session of Parliament convened at the abbey of Haddington near Leith, during which a new marriage scheme was proposed that would further unite France and Scotland. In fact, the French king, Henry II, wrote to the estates, or ruling nobility, of Scotland, requesting them to send their deputies to Paris for the wedding of Queen Mary and his son, the "dauphin," or crown prince, Francis II. Parliament voted unanimously in favor of the union, primarily because Henry II promised to defend the Scots against the English.

The court, in the midst of which Mary Stuart had grown up, was then the most magnificent, the most elegant, the most joyous, and we must add, one of the most lax, in Europe.
—FRANÇOIS MIGNET
French historian

Mary quickly became a favorite of the rich, luxurious Valois court, where she reveled in the attention she received as queen of Scotland. Later in her life Mary would try to recapture the happiness of her French childhood.

GIRAUDON/ART RESOURCE

King Henry II of France, whose court was one of the finest in Europe. Henry welcomed Mary to the French court as a means of gaining a foothold in Scotland. The French king planned to unite Mary and his son and heir, Francis, thereby creating a solid Franco-Scottish Catholic alliance.

Through this marriage, they thought, Scotland's independence would be guaranteed.

Mary took with her to France a small Scottish court: two lords, two half brothers, her governess, and four girlfriends — Mary Beaton, Mary Seaton, Mary Livingston, and Mary Fleming — all five years old, like the queen. These daughters of Scottish nobles were considered special simply because they were named Mary.

The French court of Henry II Valois was one of the most magnificent in all of Europe. In the Château St. Germain, on the edge of the beautiful forest of Lyda, Mary became the favorite of the court of Valois. Her French maids dressed her in splendid velvet, satin, and silk gowns. Veils and ribbons adorned her auburn hair, and precious jewels decorated her hands and neck (eventually the young queen would own over 180 pieces of jewelry). Her chambers were styled in the finest French decor, with chests made of sparkling jewels, mirrors of ebony and gold, and a carved, canopied bed covered with embroidered feather pillows.

King Henry II, a great patron of the arts, was also able to offer Mary the finest education available. She learned several languages — Latin, French, Spanish, and Italian — and studied such thinkers as Plato, Cicero, and Erasmus. She was instructed in verse by the famous poet Pierre de Ronsard and became a fine student of the harp and the harpsichord. Her skills at horsemanship and needlework were also developed here. As a great lover of the outdoors and animals, Mary would often display her pet falcon before the French nobles, retrieving it with the skill of a great falconer. Even as a young girl, Mary took part in the royal stag hunts. From this idyllic childhood, Mary grew to be an educated, elegant, and strong young woman who was well prepared for her future role as queen.

But Mary could not rule until she was of age. In 1554, when Mary was 12, Marie de Guise and the Parlement of Paris determined that the young queen of Scots could officially reign, even though she lived in France. The regency was taken from the earl of Arran and awarded, in Mary's name, to the queen mother, who began to create a French "satellite" in Scotland.

The change in political power and orientation did not sit well with the Scots. Protestants in the country were growing in number, and they refused to be ruled by the French Catholics appointed by the queen mother; in addition, Catholic nobles objected on the grounds of Scottish patriotism. At one point, the leader of the Scottish Protestants, John Knox, exclaimed, "It is as just to put a crown on the head of Marie de Guise as to put a saddle on the back of an unruly cow!" In 1557 the "First Covenant" of the Protestant "Lords of the Congregation" was passed, in which numerous Protestant Scottish lords grouped together and agreed to devote their lives to

Plato (left) and Aristotle were two of the most famous philosophers of classical Greece. At the French court Mary's education included the study of classical philosophers, as well as contemporary thinkers such as Erasmus, as part of her richly cultural upbringing.

Caricature by German painter Hans Holbein depicting the selling of "indulgences," or certificates of salvation, a practice much criticized by the Protestant reformers. While Mary was in France, in her native Scotland the Protestants, led by John Knox, were making significant inroads. The stage was being set for the conflict in which Mary would soon play so pivotal a role.

promoting Calvinism, a Lutheran offshoot, in their homeland, and to defeating the powerful French Catholics in Scotland. The alliance with France was severely threatened.

The French had to act quickly to secure their ties with Scotland. On April 19, 1558, in the Louvre palace, Mary Stuart and the Dauphin Francis Valois stood before the cardinal of Lorraine, Mary's uncle. The proper papers were prepared and the marriage contract was signed. The public ceremony and celebrations were to occur five days later at Nôtre Dame Cathedral.

On the evening before her wedding, Mary, a tall girl of 15, stood with her lavish white wedding gown, which was richly embroidered with rare gems. (By her wedding Mary had grown to the astounding height of almost six feet.) Beside it her violet train stretched almost across the entire chamber. Standing in front of the mirror, Mary was captivated by her gold crown sparkling in the evening sun, its sapphires, emeralds, rubies, and diamonds reflecting scintillating rainbows in the looking glass. Behind the colors Mary saw her own pale face. Before the next sunset, she, the queen of the Scots, would become the bride of the heir to the kingdom of France.

A loud heralding of trumpets the following morning announced the commencement of the day's activities. The wedding took place on April 24, 1558. The parade that preceded the bride and groom to the canopy before the great cathedral was unending. It seemed as if all of Paris had gathered to watch the royal procession — the minstrels playing their viols and horns, the lively jesters, the 100 nobles of the French court dressed in the official red and yellow, and the Scottish guests marching in their colorful plaid kilts. Tambourines and song preceded the great cardinals of the Catholic church. Finally, the 14-year-old Prince Francis arrived at the blue

Francis II Valois, the dauphin (crown prince) of France. He was only 14, and Mary a year older, when the two were married in 1558. A year later Henry II died and Francis ascended to the French throne.

pavilion, followed by his bride-to-be, Mary, queen of Scots. This was perhaps the finest hour of Mary's young life. To her right, she held the arm of King Henry II of France. To her left marched the cardinal of Lorraine. Catherine de Médicis, queen of France, and others in the royal party followed her velvet train, which was so laden with jewels that a dozen maids were needed to carry it. A silken canopy shaded the couple and silence fell over the crowd as the two young royals said their vows. The cardinal blessed the union, and the marriage was official.

After attending mass in the cathedral, Mary, Francis, and hundreds of royal guests celebrated in the bishop's palace. To honor the new queen, King Henry ordered two lords to hold her crown over her head as she dined. Mary danced with the king and her new husband beneath a ceiling of glowing chandeliers. For the new bride, the day seemed to have no end.

But Mary's happiness was not to last for very long. Dark days threatened her Scottish homeland. The Protestant nobles, gathering their forces against the rule of the Catholic queen mother, were gaining great power. In 1559 the War of the Reformation broke out. French soldiers defended the Catholic Marie de Guise, while English soldiers fought on the side of the nobles. The English were particularly concerned that any large-scale success by the French would increase the likelihood of their then mounting a full-fledged invasion of England.

In June 1560, in the midst of the turbulence, Marie de Guise died. The Protestants, led by John Knox, took this opportunity to call a "Reformation Parliament." In August they declared that the pope no longer held any power in their land and that attending a Catholic Mass was an official crime. The Reformation had finally been accomplished in Scotland.

Mary was overwhelmed by her mother's death and the actions of the lords. "I am your Queen," she wrote, "or so you call me! But you do not use me. You have done what pleased yourselves!"

Mary's ill luck had only just begun. King Henry II had died on July 10, 1559, leaving Francis and Mary

Mary's marriage to Francis II gave her not only affection but the prospect of two kingdoms. Although it was a political match, the alliance seems to have pleased Mary.

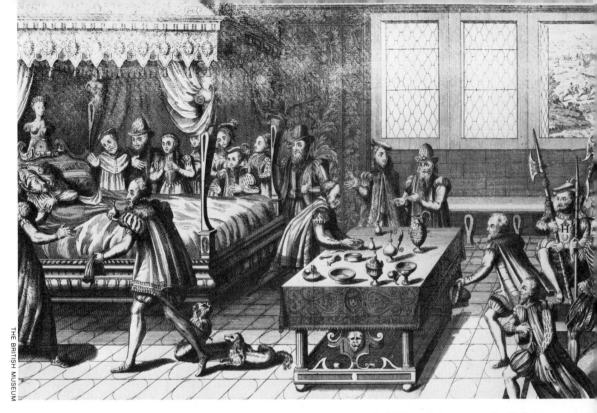

to rule as king and queen. But on December 5, 1560, after only one year on the throne together, Mary was left a widow — at the age of 17.

Henry's second son, Charles IX, replaced his brother Francis II as king. Without her sovereign husband, Mary sensed that her home was no longer in the court of Valois. Looking toward her Scottish realm she saw nothing but violence and possible misfortune should she choose to return. Her dilemma, she felt, was the most profound one she had yet faced.

But Mary had one last hope to rule. The Catholic French had long been contesting her cousin Elizabeth's right to the English throne. Elizabeth had acceded to the throne after Henry VIII's other heirs, Elizabeth's half brother, Edward VI, and half sister, Mary I, died in 1553 and 1558. The French felt that the marriage between Henry VIII and Anne Boleyn, Elizabeth's parents, was illegal because Rome had denied Henry's request for an annulment of his first marriage. Thus, reasoned the French, Elizabeth was illegitimate and Mary was the true queen of England. Elizabeth's being a Protestant certainly did not help her case, especially in Mary's eyes.

A 16th-century woodcut depicting the French royal family gathered around the deathbed of King Henry II, who had been mortally wounded in a joust. Henry's death in 1559 and Francis's a year later left Mary adrift — she no longer felt part of the French court, and she was far from her Scottish homeland as well.

4

The Mists of the Lowlands

On August 14, 1561, four royal ships set sail from Calais, France. The tall sails of the largest galley were brilliantly white in the high noon sun. The flags of the smaller red ship flapped wildly in the stormy summer winds, a blue flag on the port side bearing the heraldic arms of the French court. The Scottish queen was sailing back to her homeland.

Mary looked wearily over the choppy waters to her northern realm. For 40 days the widow had secluded herself in her bedchamber, leaving only for the funeral of her late husband. But in the many months since the loss of her mother, her husband, and her father-in-law, Mary had changed from the charming girl of the Valois court to a maturing woman and queen whose forced solitude had become her deepest strength.

New suitors were already vying for the widow's affections. Elizabeth of England feared any new alliance of Mary's; the more powerful Mary got the more likely it was that she would contest Elizabeth's throne. Of all the possible alliances, Elizabeth most

The sun was not seyn to schyne two dayis befoir, nor two dayis after. That foirwarning gave God unto us; but allace, the most pairt war blynd.
—JOHN KNOX
leader of the Scottish Protestants, on Mary's return to Scotland

As Mary sailed for troubled Scotland in 1561, she gazed sadly toward the receding shores of France, feeling a widow's grief and a concern for her future. Having left her native land as an infant, Mary hardly remembered Scotland. She was faced with the formidable task of bringing peace to her deeply divided people.

Marie de Guise was a French princess and a staunch Catholic. Until Mary came of legal age to claim the Scottish throne, Marie de Guise ruled in her daughter's name as regent. Her death in 1560 enabled Scotland's Protestants to proclaim a "Reformation Parliament" and outlaw Catholic ceremonies — making Mary's position upon her return extremely tenuous.

feared Mary's considered marriage to Don Carlos, heir apparent to the Spanish throne; it was said that Spain would invade England on Mary's behalf, prompting Elizabeth to warn Mary that going through with this match would be considered a declaration of war. Catherine de Médicis, Mary's mother-in-law, was also against the union, thinking that it would raise Mary's stature (and that of the de Guise family) at the expense of Catherine and her family. Furthermore, the Spanish heir himself said he would not wed the young queen while her kingdom was in such turmoil. Finally, Mary also needed the consent of the estates of Scotland, an unlikely prospect given the deeply divided feelings that pervaded the country. She was left with no choice but to return to her strife-worn homeland and try to negotiate peace.

Mary had not seen the Lowlands in 13 years. Few friends remained in the largely Protestant land. Even her Catholic subjects were wary of her arrival. An agent from Edinburgh warned of a Protestant rebellion against the queen: "When she comes here it will be a mad world. Their exactness and singularity in religion will never concur with her judgment!" The fiery Protestant preacher John Knox publicly condemned Mary as a "new harlot, Jezebel!"

Even her half brother James Stuart, the earl of Moray, took up arms with her enemies. James had never forgiven her for taking the throne from him. Although they had the same father, young James was illegitimate and therefore could never rightfully wear the crown. James was ruthless in his revenge and fervent Protestantism, fighting against Marie de Guise while she was alive and even fraternizing with Mary's worst enemy, Queen Elizabeth. Obviously, Mary could never trust James, but perhaps he could serve as an invaluable liaison with the Scottish Protestants. Another Protestant statesman, the clever but moderate William Maitland of Lethington, would also be a valuable adviser. Maitland backed Mary despite their religious differences because he was a pragmatist and because he believed in a peaceful union between Scotland and England. Mary had seen James at Joinville, France, before embarking for Scotland. He was watching her closely to calculate her plans for the divided kingdom.

Every power in Europe — the Catholic church, the Reformation leaders, Elizabeth in England, Don Carlos in Spain, and the new French King Charles IX — was waiting to see what actions the young Mary would take. Would the Catholic queen tolerate a Protestant religion in her realm? Would her subjects tolerate another Catholic ruler, particularly one raised in France?

The French question was more pressing. Before marrying Francis II, Mary had secretly signed a document ceding Scotland to the French in the event of her death or the absence of an heir. Although the French began as mere protectors of Scotland against England, they had, with the help of Marie de Guise, assumed a powerful role in the country's affairs — too powerful, in the eyes of many Scots. The patriotic northerners, for instance, did not want yet another French import ruling their beloved country. For Mary's Protestant subjects, however, it was not the invasion of foreigners that mattered so much as their religion. As John Knox exclaimed, the threat to the country was Catholicism itself: "I would rather see 10,000 French soldiers landed in Scotland, than suffer a single Catholic Mass!"

When Mary's ship reached Scotland, few people were on hand to greet their queen. Even her half brother James Stuart had joined the Protestants, who now dominated the country.

An earlier attempt to deal with the problem and to end the civil war that followed Marie de Guise's death had produced the Treaty of Edinburgh in July 1560, drawn up just before Francis's death, in which Catholic pro-French and Protestant nationalists agreed that all foreign troops were to be withdrawn from Scotland. The treaty's other main proviso was that Mary and Francis refrain from acknowledging themselves as heirs to the English throne. But Mary refused to ratify the treaty, before and after her return to Scotland. She would not recognize Elizabeth's right to rule. The English crown, she felt more and more, was hers to claim.

Mary's refusal to endorse the Treaty of Edinburgh prompted Elizabeth to deny her safe overland passage through England to the north for the journey home from France. Thus, a more risky sea voyage was necessary, with a sailor posted high in the crow's nest of Mary's French ship to keep a keen watch for any threatening English vessels. When the lookout was able to sight the coastal town of Leith in the distance, its red-tiled houses were almost totally obscured by a dense mist covering sea and shore. Scotland was not to offer itself easily to the returning sovereign.

Because the ships had found strong winds to sail, they reached the shores of Scotland much sooner than expected, and no delegation was there at the landing stage to greet Mary. Soon, however, her half brother James arrived, albeit with a cool welcome; the earl of Arran's greeting was no warmer. Used to the lavish attentions of the French court, Mary was a bit dismayed by the meager audience.

The modest welcoming celebrations of the following days also paled next to the customs of St. Germain. As small bonfires spotted Calton Hill and Salisbury Crags, telegraphing the news of her arrival from village to village, and mobs of peasants crowded the lumbering horses and carriages of the royal procession, Mary slowly made her way to Edinburgh, her future home. Whatever disappointment or trepidation Mary was feeling was eased by the fact that the people of Edinburgh were indeed glad to greet their elegant queen. Her royal bearing and

GIRAUDON/ART RESOURCE

Catherine de Médicis of Florence, Mary's mother-in-law. After her husband Henry II's death, Catherine sought to remain politically influential in France. Catherine closely monitored Mary's possible marriage alliances; she wanted to make certain Mary made no match that would eclipse the power of the de Médicis family.

rich silks were quite impressive in the dirty streets of the capital.

Mary's home was to be at Holyrood Palace, which had been the residence of many Scottish kings and queens before Mary but whose main buildings had not been restored since the bloody wars of the rough wooing. Mary saw this as a chance to recreate the splendor of her French homeland. She had the floors covered with colorful Turkish carpets, and had heavy tapestries hung over the walls to cut down on damp drafts. She had her rooms decorated with the finest marble and gold furnishings, and had jeweled chandeliers installed in every room. But despite her efforts, the cold and dark palace never equalled the French castle of her youth.

John Knox, Scotland's Protestant leader, admonishing Mary shortly after her return. His belief that Scotland would never be at peace under Catholic rule sounded like treason to Mary; indeed, for the next several years Knox and Mary engaged in a relentless duel for supremacy in the country.

39

Mary encounters David Riccio, an Italian court musician, at the bottom of a staircase in the royal palace at Holyrood. The two became close friends; Riccio's entertaining conversation took the queen's mind off her country's troubles and his songs soothed her spirit.

One of Mary's first tasks as queen was to meet with the troublesome leader of the Protestant opposition, John Knox, who in 1558 had published an attack against Mary and the Catholic church called *A First Blast of the Trumpet against the Monstrous Regiment of Women*. Mary tried to reason with Knox, but finally openly accused him of treasonous organizing. Mary wanted to let both religions coexist peacefully in Scotland, but Knox was convinced that neither of the two factions would ever tolerate compromise. Scotland had weathered civil wars in the past, he reasoned, and Mary must get used to the idea that more conflicts would occur in the future; with a Catholic sovereign in a Protestant country, there would never be peace.

In her own councils, however, Mary argued against such extremism and instead tried to represent both religions fairly. Seven of her councilors were Protestant, and five were Catholic. Nevertheless, arguments and divisions were unending, even among coreligionists, and particularly between the earl of Arran and James Hepburn, the fourth earl of Bothwell.

Like Arran, Bothwell was a Protestant, although he was a man with few allegiances, political or religious, other than those that would serve his own personal advancement. Mary was attracted to Bothwell, as he was an educated, confident, and decisive man. Mary saw him as an answer to an immediate problem; her splintered country beckoned for leadership.

Mary spent the first months of her reign exploring and rediscovering her kingdom. She rode from castle to cathedral, disturbed by the unending discord she saw between Catholics and Protestants. Back in Edinburgh, Mary alleviated her troubled spirit with music, dance, and feasting. Bothwell and Mary's half brothers John and Robert entertained the maids of her court with late nights of revelry. Her dear friend and adviser, David Riccio, stayed up late with Mary, playing Italian melodies on his lute and passing the night hours with card games. Mary seems to have temporarily deluded herself that her true reign of peace had begun.

Mary was in many respects the antithesis of her cousin the queen of England. Brought up at the Court of France, at that time the most brilliant and gayest in christendom, she had enjoyed a comparatively sheltered existence, unharassed by the grim experience that had shaped and disciplined the character of Anne Boleyn's daughter.
—J.B. BLACK
British historian

5

Wars and Weddings

Mary had not forgotten her plans for the English throne. Lord James and Secretary Maitland advised her to cultivate a friendship with England, believing that an alliance would prompt Elizabeth to name Mary as her successor. But most Catholics — particularly George Gordon, the fourth earl of Huntly, who was the most powerful Catholic in Scotland — strongly opposed Scotland's flirting with a Protestant country. Gordon ruled the Scottish Highlands of the north, and claimed the earldom of Moray. Backed by the northern Catholics and the wealth of many castles, lands, and herds, the rebellious earl was willing to instigate an uprising to prevent Mary's allegiance with England.

Mary decided to pay the earl a diplomatic visit. As she rode toward the northern moorlands on August 11, 1562, she prepared herself to encounter Huntly's armies, since an armed confrontation between the two headstrong leaders was a distinct possibility. Beside her rode her brother James, who desperately coveted the earldom of Moray, which Huntly had administered (but did not officially hold) since 1549. Both Mary and James were well aware that the earl's overthrow would serve two purposes: it

Nursed from her infancy in a blind attachment to the Roman Catholic religion, every means had been employed before she left France to strengthen this prejudice, and to inspire her with aversion to the religion which had been embraced by her people.
—THOMAS McCRIE
19th-century historian

Mary in 1562. At the time the choice of a second husband was a serious political problem for the young sovereign. The Catholic queen needed to find a royal suitor who would both satisfy her own religious convictions and be acceptable to the Protestant Scottish lords.

James Stuart, earl of Moray, Mary's half brother. James won his earldom for supporting Mary against the powerful earl of Huntly. The Protestant Moray would continue to aid Mary only as long as it was to his own advantage.

would advance Mary's efforts for the English crown while placating the Scottish Protestants, and it would win the rich earldom of Moray for James. (Unbeknownst to the earl, Lord James had secretly secured the title to the earldom in January.) Mary had decided that if she had to fight this "cock o' the north," she would; she could not show partiality in her kingdom — both Catholics and Protestants must be subject to her royal authority.

On the evening of September 10, 1562, Mary reached the earl's mansion of Darnaway, where she announced that James would henceforth be the earl of Moray. The small royal troop journeyed the next day to Inverness Castle, another Gordon possession, but its gates were barred to the queen by the keeper of the castle. Mary, however, eventually gained entrance to the castle and installed herself as rightful ruler of the region. She then used this power base to mount a challenge to the earl, who was entrenched but increasingly on the defensive at his Strathbogie stronghold.

Rumors were running rampant; the most often heard one was that the Huntlys — the earl and two of his sons — were gathering for an attack. Finally, on October 28, 700 Highlanders, Huntly's clansmen, attacked the queen's forces, which had by then grown to 3,000 men. With blasting trumpets and clashing broadswords, Mary's army drove the northerners into the marshy fields of Corrichie, 15 miles west of Aberdeen. James's army overwhelmed the opposition, killing hundreds and capturing Huntly's two sons, John and Adam. Huntly himself had died from a seizure in the heat of the battle.

Mary was ecstatic at her triumph. "I never saw her merrier!" one lord wrote. The young queen considered regretfully that "she was not a man to know what life it was to lie all night in the fields, or to walk upon the causeway with a jack and a knapscall [iron skullcap], a Glasgow buckler, and a broadsword!" Mary had now shown herself to be a strong Scottish queen, sure of her policies and her battlefield prowess. Huntly was defeated, the spoils of the earldom of Moray were passed to Mary and James, the chances for peace in the Scottish kingdom ap-

peared greater, and the English throne was closer than ever.

Of chief importance to the question of the English succession was who would be Mary's next husband. If Elizabeth was to grant Mary her crown, then it was only right that the English queen be consulted as to whom Mary should wed.

With Mary securely on her Scottish throne, the Spanish King Philip II had begun to seek Mary's possible union with his heir, Don Carlos. But Elizabeth, fearing war, was against the match, as were Catherine de Médicis, the pope, and Mary's uncle, the cardinal of Lorraine.

Once again, Mary's hopes for a great kingdom were dashed. The cardinal secretly agreed to wed Mary to Archduke Charles, the uncle of Don Carlos. But Mary was not about to settle — she wanted to be queen of Spain, not to be one of its court maids. Since a Spanish union appeared out of the question, Mary set her sights again on England. Eliza-

Inverness Castle, which dominates the central city of the Scottish Highlands, belonged to George Gordon, earl of Huntly. Huntly, a Catholic, opposed Mary's attempts to form an alliance with Protestant England. As a show of authority, Mary captured the castle as a prelude to breaking Huntly's power in the north.

beth had even told Maitland of Lethington — who was involved in the various marital negotiations — that if Mary married to Elizabeth's satisfaction she would be named the English queen's rightful successor. Mary realized she had to secure Elizabeth's consent to a groom and then slowly plan to take over the English crown.

The only suitor Elizabeth suggested was Lord Robert Dudley, the earl of Leicester, who had been her own previous lover. Mary was presented with the proposal on March 5, 1564, but six months later the young queen was still undecided. Elizabeth, angry with Mary for not ratifying the Treaty of Edinburgh and thereby acknowledging Elizabeth's sovereignty, offered no further help.

Tuaghs, or Scottish battle-axes. Mary's resounding 1562 victory over Huntly at Corrichie not only gave her increased political confidence but showed her to be a strong field commander willing to pursue with force a course of action she thought right for her country.

Henry Stuart, Lord Darnley, four years younger than his cousin Mary, was the perfect suitor in her eyes. His handsome, boyish face, blue eyes, and golden hair set her heart ablaze. Also, she believed she would stand a better chance of succession to the throne if married to an English heir.

Finally, in the autumn of 1564, Elizabeth took an important step (that would ultimately prove disastrous for Mary). She persuaded Mary to allow Matthew Stuart, earl of Lennox, who had been banished from Scotland for allying himself with the English, and his eldest son, 19-year-old Henry Stuart, Lord Darnley, to return to Scotland. Darnley was also an English heir; Mary and he shared the same grandmother, Margaret Tudor, sister of Henry VIII. The English queen's motives are unclear, even mysterious. Perhaps she thought she could use the opportunity of a possible marriage between Darnley and Mary as an excuse not to name any clear successor to the English throne. Or, being unaware that the negotiations for a wedding to the Spanish prince had ended, Elizabeth was trying to dissuade Mary from marrying Don Carlos, easing the threat of war. In either scenario, it is evident that Elizabeth thought that her position as queen would be more secure with Darnley as Mary's husband.

Mary saw things differently. She thought she would have an even greater chance for succession if she married the English heir. Mary considered Darnley the perfect suitor. She had heard that he was well educated and had all the elegance of the English court. Even more, he was handsome, with golden hair and blue eyes. Although Darnley, technically a Catholic, gave heed to the Calvinist teachings of Knox, his mother was a devout Catholic. The royal Tudor blood flowed through both of them. Surely, Mary hoped, marrying such a man would mean the English crown would soon be in her grasp.

David Riccio, Mary's court confidant, urged Mary to wed Lord Darnley. "Davie," as Mary called him, wanted to see the Catholic kingdom revived in the land, and considered the handsome Darnley a good, strong companion and consort for his dear friend Mary. All of Mary's other statesmen, however, advised her against the marriage, saying that she had

Be governor both good and gracious
Be loyal and loving to thy lieges all.
—HENRY STUART,
LORD DARNLEY
from a poem written for Mary

Elizabeth's royal autograph. The "R" after her name stood for "Regina" or "Queen." Elizabeth, who more than anyone stood to gain or lose by Mary's choice of husband, feared that Mary might choose a French or Spanish Catholic,who would then invade England on her behalf to claim the English throne.

Margaret Tudor, the sister of King Henry VIII, was Mary's grandmother and Elizabeth's aunt. The Tudors had been the English royal family since 1485. Another of Margaret's descendants, Henry Stuart, would play a crucial role in Mary's life.

fallen blindly for Darnley's charms and veneer. Lord James, now the earl of Moray, and Maitland of Lethington thought Darnley immature. Certainly they acknowledged he was a fine sportsman, musician, and dancer, but a king he was not. Other members of the royal entourage found him to be weak, malicious, and treacherous. Historians have suggested that Elizabeth had known all along about Darnley's questionable character. Nonetheless, Mary was intent on the marriage. She resisted any attempts to make her the pawn for some diplomatic liaisons and was determined to marry whomever she chose.

In February 1565 Lord Darnley began his courtship. One evening, the earl of Moray invited some guests to his home for wine, music, and dance. Mary and Lord Darnley glided over the polished floors, Mary infatuated with Darnley's charms. Seeing her satin gown glowing in the candlelight reminded Mary of the royal courts of her youth. How proud she was to be in the strong arms of such a gallant man. Darnley was very attractive — he has been described as looking like a young god — but he was also four years Mary's junior, and his immaturity and childish pride would soon surface. When it did, Mary would finally realize the mistake she had made in following her heart and passion against the best interests of the country.

6

Irrevocable Error

At 6:00 A.M. on July 29, 1565, a hooded woman walked slowly through the gloomy halls of Holyrood Palace. Her mourning gown trailed behind her on the cold stones. She was followed by two earls, whose downcast expressions were not those normally associated with a wedding party. Mary, queen of Scots, turned to stand before the wedding altar in the small chapel beside her castle. For a brief moment, she thought of the bright blue pavilion outside the grand Nôtre Dame Cathedral and the glory of her first wedding. But here in Scotland there were no joyous multitudes or bagpipes playing. Her reverie broken, she stood alone as a widow, awaiting her fiancé, Henry Stuart, Lord Darnley.

The earls ushered in the young lord, and together the couple knelt before the priest as the morning light shone through the stained glass above them.

Mary had taken great risks in deciding to wed Lord Darnley. In marrying a Catholic, she was alienating her powerful Protestant nobles and defying

> *Although she excelled in courtly accomplishments and conformed in the main to courtly conventions, she was at heart a free spirit with much of the freshness, simplicity, and abandon of a wild thing about her.*
> —CONYERS READ
> British historian, on Mary

Mary and her husband, Lord Darnley. Mary had chosen her husband against the wishes of most of her advisers, and she married him hastily before any opposition could intervene. Not long after the bleak wedding ceremony, so lacking the pomp of her first marriage, Mary would come to know the true nature of her spiteful husband.

Queen Elizabeth, who had, in an apparent change of opinion, made known her disapproval of the marriage and consequently announced that no heir would be named for the English throne. Mary had also provoked the anger of her jealous brother James. The young queen, however, had grown gen-

Elizabeth I ruled England for 45 years. Many of the Scottish Protestant lords who opposed Mary and Darnley turned to Elizabeth, seeking aid for an insurrection. Elizabeth shrewdly kept Mary guessing as to how much support England was actually willing to offer the Scottish noblemen.

John Knox was extremely upset about Mary's marriage to the Catholic Lord Darnley. Although the celebrations following the wedding were sparse in comparison to Mary's French ceremony, Knox complained that for "three or four days, there was nothing but balling, and dancing and banqueting."

uinely fond of Darnley. Mary's insistence on a quick marriage was not due to passion alone; strong political forces were gathering to prevent the Catholic union. She had to act quickly, or the wedding might never happen.

Before the altar, Darnley gave Mary three rings for her hand and kissed his new wife and queen. As was the custom, Mary laid aside her widow's gar-

John Calvin, the 16th-century French theologian and leading Protestant reformer. The Scottish Protestants were greatly influenced by Calvinism. This austere, uncompromising faith was established in Scotland by Knox, and it provided the basis for modern-day Scottish Presbyterianism.

THE BETTMANN ARCHIVE

ments and donned the bright colors of a new bride. The meager dancing and feasting that followed only served as another bitter reminder of what had gone before — the sumptuous banquets and merriment following her French wedding — when the halls overflowed with sweet wines and harmonious song. At 9:00 that evening, the bells chimed in Edinburgh and the announcement was heralded from the royal palace: In Mary's name, Henry, Lord Darnley, Lord Ardmarnock, earl of Ross, duke of Albany, had become "king of this our kingdom!" But hardly an "amen" was heard from those present.

Only six months after arriving in Scotland, Darnley had become, at least by title, the second most powerful person in the country. The Protestants feared that they had lost all hope of dominance in Scotland, despite Mary's assurances that religious freedom would be respected. Few, particularly the

Map of the British Isles. In 1565 the Scottish Protestant lords, unhappy with Mary's recent marriage, felt the time was ripe for rebellion. The earl of Moray hoped to encircle Mary's troops by marching east toward Edinburgh while English reinforcements pressed northward, but his plan soon went awry.

earl of Moray, recognized the authority of the new king. In fact, James was desperate. For four years he had been the quasi-king of Scotland. Not only was he now battling to retain his power over his half sister, but the presence of a Catholic king — even one who was not particularly outspoken about his religion — threatened the Protestants of the Reformation. He decided to foment an uprising to signal his discontent with the queen and the marriage.

James had been carefully watching the royal couple for several weeks, beginning well before the wedding. By mid-August 1565 his plan was ready: he would enlist the support of Queen Elizabeth, crush the insolent Darnley, his foolish queen, and their Catholic followers, and proclaim himself ruler of Scotland. From Ayr, Argyll, Glencairn, and the surrounding towns he would gather Protestant lords ready to support him, led by the strong Scottish general, William Kirkcaldy of Grange. To the south, on the English border, James's ally, the duke of Bedford, waited with his troops. Together, the armies would converge on Edinburgh and take the queen's castle. On the eve of his rebellion, the earl of Moray was pleased with himself. His plot looked flawless.

The thunder of dissent soon reached Mary's court, and the queen wasted no time in rallying her supporters. She called for the release from prison of Huntly's eldest son, Lord George Gordon, whom Mary had imprisoned after the defeat of his father's forces in the Highlands. She also issued a proclamation to her subjects: "That forasmuch certain Rebels, who (under the colour of religion) intended nothing but the trouble and subversion of the Commonwealth, were to convene with such as they might persuade to assist them; therefore they [Mary and Darnley] charged all manner of men, under pain of life, lands, and goods, to resort and meet their Majesties at Linlithgow, the twenty-fourth day of August."

Hundreds of armed peasants united on the queen's side. On August 26 she led an army of 800

A crossbowman of the Scots guards winding up his bow. Other weapons and equipment carried by soldiers of the time included wood-and-leather shields, "dirks," which were short daggers, and pistols. Soldiers' allegiances were identified by the colors and patterns on their kilts.

men from Edinburgh through Stirling and Linlithgow. By the time her troops arrived at Glasgow, their numbers had risen to over 5,000 soldiers.

Moray's armies rode for days avoiding Mary's mighty troops. This "run-about-raid" took his soldiers through Paisley, Hamilton, and finally into Edinburgh. Moray's troops amounted to only 1,300 men, as Elizabeth had retracted her promise of military support. Moreover, the Protestants of the capital failed to flock to Moray's side, a severe blow to the spirit of Moray's insurrection. The earl of Mar, commanding the queen's army in Edinburgh, opened fire on the Protestant soldiers. Meanwhile, Mary's legions were quickly approaching.

The chase continued. Mary's troops were soon joined by the earl of Bothwell, who had escaped from prison, where he had been sent for committing a minor crime. Mary's forces, sensing a rout, were prepared for a slaughter. Moray left quickly for Lanark and Dumfries to the south, and continued to entreat the aid of Elizabeth. The English queen, however, continued to withhold her support. She had also received a note from her Scottish cousin

The coat of arms of Scotland's largest city, Glasgow. The "run-about-raid," in which Moray's men rode through many cities, including Glasgow, to avoid an encounter with the royal forces, ended in an overwhelming victory for Mary.

LET GLASGOW FLOURISH

stating: "Madame, my sister: I understand you are offended without just cause against the King my husband and myself; and what is worse, your servants on the Border threaten to burn and plunder our subjects who wish to aid us against our rebels. If it please you to make your cause that of our traitors, which I cannot believe, we shall be compelled not to conceal it from our princely allies."

Moray's troops, without the allegiance of England, were powerless before Mary's forces. They soon disbanded, the earl fleeing to England and the court of the unfaithful Elizabeth; he had nowhere else to turn. Moray's failed rebellion was a significant triumph for Mary — she again showed herself to be a strong military leader, willing to enlist thousands to protect her right to wed Darnley. The victory even prompted Mary to state that her army would soon march successfully on London.

Tragically, however, the weak king was hardly worthy of his faithful wife. Mary began to see that perhaps her fighting had been in vain, that she was protecting a selfish, power-hungry child who demanded the full rights, but lacked the character, of a sovereign. Darnley drank constantly, insulted Mary before her court, and avoided the responsibilities of his kingship. He was even suspected of having illicit affairs with men in the court. Particularly galling to Mary in her conduct of affairs of state was that she had to have Henry's signature sealed in a stamp because he was absent so often.

Despite his despicable conduct, Darnley constantly demanded the "crown matrimonial" — the full rights to the crown — which would secure power for himself and his heirs in the event of Mary's death. Prudently, Mary granted her husband no such power, and neither would her advisers.

Soon Darnley's title fell from "king consort" to "the queen's husband." He had become a mere appendage, a useless associate of the dominant Queen Mary. Darnley, however, could still wield much influence in a court already divided by religious controversy. Jealous of the power he could never own, the angry young ruler began plotting to take his "rightful" throne by force.

The royal authority in her own Kingdom, she would divide with no party, no minister, no husband.
—THOMAS ROBERTSON
18th-century historian

7

Blood and Betrayal

During the run-about-raid, Moray issued a proc-lamation explaining that he had taken arms against the throne because, by her marriage, Mary was not only threatening the Protestant faith but was also neglecting the counsel of her closest advisers, re-lying instead on "strangers . . . men of base degree." One of the base advisers Moray was referring to was Mary's trustworthy companion and court musician, David Riccio.

A Catholic, Riccio was suspected by the Protestant court of being a foreign spy for the Italian pope. What's more, Darnley suspected he and Mary were carrying on an affair. Indeed, in her private secre-tary the queen had found the friendship and con-fidence that was lacking in her marriage. Mary and David often kept each other company until the early morning hours, but no evidence has been found indicating an affair. Nevertheless, the jealous con-sort would no longer allow the intrusive Riccio in his courts. Mary vehemently disagreed and the issue became a sore point between them.

The murder of Riccio marks the turning point in Mary's career, both personally and politically. The character of her husband had been laid bare; henceforth she could feel for him nothing but contempt and loathing.
—MAURICE LEE
British historian

In what has been called the turning point of Mary's reign, on March 9, 1566, Mary's beloved companion David Ric-cio was murdered in her presence, and the queen, preg-nant at the time, was made a prisoner in her own palace. Darnley, her weak, frustrated husband, was implicated in the murder.

A gateway to Holyrood Palace in Edinburgh. The imprisoned Mary, fearing for her life, realized that her only chance of escape was to convince Darnley that the rebel lords would soon turn against him as well.

Finally, Darnley began to conspire with England and the Scottish lords who had fled the country following their involvement in the run-about-raid. Mary had declared that those supporters of Moray were to be "forfeited in life, lands, and goods." A session of Parliament was scheduled for March 12, 1566, that would decide their fate. The banished lords, fearing the queen's punishment, were willing to pledge their full support to the king's conspiracy in exchange for his protection.

Although the exiled Moray promised Darnley the crown matrimonial and succession to the Scottish throne, Moray was only humoring the gullible king. He and the lords planned to use Darnley to regain their power, and then, having no more need of him, would demote him to court jester or even have him killed. The unsuspecting Darnley was lulled into believing that the Protestant rebels were uniting behind him to elevate him to his rightful position as sovereign. But just as this plot to destroy his wife was set to go forward, another destructive series of events ensued.

On the evening of March 9, 1566, Mary sat dining in her private chambers with six nobles. The countess of Argyll and Lord Robert Stuart were at her side. Riccio sat opposite her in his gay, feathered hat, strumming upon his lute. Mary, six months pregnant with Darnley's child, accompanied Riccio's Italian love songs with sweet humming, as the gathered nobility feasted on delicate meats and red wines.

Meanwhile, at the gates of Holyrood Palace, 300 armed men had assembled. At their head was Lord Darnley, holding a dagger high; the idea of murdering the queen's "lover" excited a weak smile across his face. He was determined to end the influence of the untrustworthy Italian minister.

Darnley climbed the queen's private stairway, opened the door, and beheld Mary and her guests. Drunk, he staggered across the silent room and kissed the queen on the back of her neck.

Suddenly the room filled with brandished knives and loud screams; several of Darnley's other accomplices rushed in. Candles flew across the room; goblets and plates were hurled through the windows. Mary felt a pistol at her side and saw a dagger glistening at her throat. Darnley restrained the raging queen in his arms. An arm suddenly shot over Mary's shoulder. Blood ripped across her velvet cloak, and she saw Riccio being pulled across the carpet. A dagger was wedged in his back — it bore the initials of her husband.

Later, the court physician would count almost 60 knife wounds in Riccio's body. After the murderers had had their fill, they threw the corpse down the long stone staircase; the hysterical guests could clearly hear the uneven thuds as it fell to the floor below. The assailants remained scattered about the chamber, drinking wine. Mary stood alone, shaking, holding her stomach, wondering if her baby

> *Some of our subjects and council by their proceedings have declared manifestly what men they are . . . slain our most special servant in our own presence and thereafter held our proper person captive treasonably.*
> —MARY, QUEEN OF SCOTS
> from a letter to Queen Elizabeth about the murder of Riccio

was in any danger. Her husband sat slumped on the floor.

The commotion had sparked confusion in the palace, and several of the queen's servants and guards appeared at the doorway, ready to defend the queen only to be turned away by the king's men. With the palace out of her control, Mary realized she was now a prisoner in her own home.

Moray, who had clearly conspired in Riccio's murder, had returned to Edinburgh. He and the rebel lords would go unpunished. Certainly, Mary reasoned, they would stop at nothing to take her throne — even if it meant her death. Plotting an escape became her immediate concern; grief over the brutal murder would have to wait.

Darnley came to her chambers the following morning, denying all involvement in the murder. Mary could hardly believe his words. Later, she would describe her husband as "so facile that he could conceal no secret although it was to his own hurt." Darnley told Mary that she was to remain a prisoner and that she would be forced to sign full pardons for those involved with Riccio's death. The conspirators and Darnley were going to usurp Mary's government; Mary would be put under house arrest at Stirling Castle for the rest of her days.

Dunbar, as painted by J. M. W. Turner, an English painter known for his landscapes. After duping Darnley into helping her escape, Mary fled to Dunbar to be with James Hepburn, the earl of Bothwell. There she began to assemble her forces in alliance with Bothwell to defeat Moray, the leader behind the rebellion.

Mary was weak from the fighting and fearful for her baby, but what she lacked in strength she gained in cleverness. Mary began to cajole her husband, hoping to regain his allegiance and enlist his help.

Mary attempted to convince Darnley that Moray would soon betray him. In fact, she was probably accurate in predicting what the lords would have done with Darnley had they succeeded in their plans. Mary promised her full forgiveness. Darnley, a coward "with a mind like wax" (as Mary described it), changed his allegiance and agreed to help Mary.

Before the sun rose on March 12, Darnley and a young page mounted two steeds and rode past the gates of Holyrood Palace. Once outside the city limits, the page removed the disguise: Mary, queen of Scots, was holding the reins. Darnley, believing Mary's promise that the two of them would rule equally, had spirited her to freedom. Mary, however, had different plans.

The two rode through the Scottish countryside to Dunbar Castle, home of James Hepburn, the earl of

In March 1566 Mary, with the aid of Bothwell and his followers, again defeated Moray and regained power in Edinburgh. Moray fled to England, and Darnley became discredited as a murderer and a traitor in both Protestant and Catholic eyes.

65

Mary with her son, James, who was born in June 1566. As his mother had been, the infant James was hidden away at Stirling Castle for protection. Mary hoped that James would someday reign over a united kingdom of Scotland and England.

Bothwell. Bothwell had been one of the targets of the Riccio murder plot but had managed to escape during the confusion. Since the run-about-raid Bothwell had become one of Mary's closest ministers. Now that Riccio was dead, Mary turned completely to Bothwell for advice and support. Rumors eventually cropped up intimating that Mary and Bothwell were lovers and that Mary was carrying not Darnley's but Bothwell's child. Historians have debated how many of Mary's unwise political decisions were actually motivated by emotional ties. Certainly her decision to ally herself with Bothwell was to have disastrous consequences.

Mary called her forces to assemble at Bothwell's castle. On March 17, 1566, the queen attacked and defeated Moray's armies for a second time. Once again, Moray and the murderers of Riccio fled to England. The following day Mary rode proudly back to Edinburgh. Having left the capital disguised as a page, she returned in the full regalia of her throne.

The murder of Riccio proved to be a turning point in Mary's reign. Having been double-crossed by Darnley, the conspirators admitted her husband's full involvement in the minister's death — an involvement Darnley had been denying to Mary. Whereas before Mary had reason to dislike her immature husband, now she hated him openly as a traitor to her crown and a threat to their unborn child. In addition, though Darnley had previously been able to garner the support of the Protestant party in Scotland, he was now a traitor in their eyes as well, having helped Mary escape and defeat their armies. Darnley was left without a single ally in all of Scotland.

The murderous intrigues of the court were temporarily forgotten, however, with the birth of Mary's child. The small nursery was well equipped. Buckets of gold and silver were imported from France, and feather pillows filled the velvet-curtained bed. Mary had special gowns of blue taffeta and silks made, and ordered 10 ells (an English unit of length equal to 45 inches) of blue Holland cloth for the newborn's cradle. James Stuart was born on June 19, 1566, in the corner room of Edinburgh Castle. A male heir

> *In proportion as her husband sunk, the Earl of Bothwell rose in her confidence and esteem.*
> —MALCOLM LAING
> British historian

A plunging falcon prepares to sink its talons into a small bird. The sport of falconry was one of the favorite pastimes of the English and Scottish nobles in the 1500s.

to the Scottish throne was reason to celebrate; indeed, some 500 bonfires lit the Scottish hills.

The birth of Prince James seemed to invest Mary with heightened conviction. On one occasion, as the 23-year-old mother lay in bed and held the small child to her breast, she turned to a lord at her side and said reverently, "This is the son who, I hope, shall first unite the two kingdoms of Scotland and England."

At eight weeks Prince James was taken to Stirling Castle for safety, where Mary had also been taken as a baby. The queen, aware of the tug-of-war that had occurred with the English during her own childhood, was taking no chances with the prince, who would indeed play a large role in uniting the two warring countries.

At six months, James celebrated his baptism at Stirling. The nobles ordered special garments for the occasion, "some in cloth of silver, some in cloth of gold, some in cloth of tissue, every man rather above than under his degree." One noble was missing, however — Lord Darnley, who soon left the capital for his home at Glasgow.

Mary received a gift for the ceremony, a gold baptismal font from James's godmother, Queen Elizabeth. Upon hearing the news of her cousin Mary's delivery, the barren English queen lamented. The long-standing rivalry between the two queens could see no end.

The rivalry between Darnley and the conspirators whom he had betrayed also could see no end. As the Edinburgh church bells loudly proclaimed the baptism of Prince James Stuart, some people felt they sounded more like a death knell, a portent of coming destruction. On Christmas Eve, a week following the baptism, Mary signed a proclamation allowing Riccio's murderers and Moray back into Scotland. It is unclear whether Mary had any inkling that by doing so she was implicitly signing Darnley's death warrant; it is clear that Mary, more and more, wanted to be rid of Darnley. Her pardon and other actions set the stage for more violence to be loosed upon the land.

MARY QUEEN OF SCOTS.

8

The Widowed Mermaid

In late January 1567 the queen's party traveled over the city roads from Glasgow to Edinburgh. In the middle of the slow-moving caravan rode a curtained "horse-litter." Inside, Lord Darnley slept, a taffeta mask about his face. Mary had retrieved her husband from his parents' hideaway, where he had been nursing a contagious illness called the "purples" — which was either smallpox or syphilis. Mary, not wanting Prince James to be exposed to disease, arranged a convalescent home for the diseased king at the broken-down collegiate church of St. Mary, called Kirk o' Field, about one mile from Holyrood Palace. In addition she arranged to have a temporary room directly under Darnley's so she could give full attention to nursing her ailing king.

On February 1 Darnley moved into his new residence. His quarters were prepared much like Holyrood, with tapestries from Strathbogie, Turkish carpets, red velvet cushions, and a gift from Mary, the special canopy bed of Marie de Guise.

The sudden change in Mary's affections puzzled the court. After Riccio's murder, Mary began to openly entertain the attentions of the earl of Bothwell. Indeed, many courtiers said they were having an affair. Why was she suddenly doting over her insolent king?

> *Plots and intrigues were the familiar weapons of the Queen of Scots.*
> —J. D. LEADER
> 19th-century historian

Even after Riccio's death, Mary continued to ignore her advisers' counsel, personal feelings still clouding her judgment. She pardoned the murderers, including Darnley, and even nursed her husband through an illness. In 1567 Mary became involved in a second disastrous relationship, one that would hasten her downfall.

An example of Mary's tapestry embroideries. In January 1567 Mary appeared a model of domesticity and devotion, raising her child and caring for the ailing Darnley. Yet rumors of an affair with Bothwell, whom Mary regularly entertained, abounded.

Bothwell had all the courage, passion, and authority that Darnley lacked. He was well educated and had traveled extensively. He also had a reputation for being a ladies' man, even during his marriage to Jean Gordon, the powerful sister of Huntly. In fact, Bothwell's family had a history of charming widowed queens for personal advancement. Bothwell's father, Patrick, known as the "fair earl," had pursued Marie de Guise after the death of King James. Bothwell, apparently, had inherited his father's ambitions. According to Lord Herries, one of Mary's contemporaries, Bothwell was a man "high in his own conceit, proud, vicious, and vainglorious above measure, one who would attempt anything out of ambition." Another noble described him as "naughty a man as liveth, and much given to detestable vices." Yet Mary was infatuated with the earl's charms.

The queen had not learned from her past mistakes. She had entered into yet another devastating liaison with a man of questionable character — a man whose ambitions were much greater than those of the weak Darnley. Bothwell and Mary had become close confidants, but at the same time Mary was acting as a loving wife and nurse to the husband who had wronged her so terribly. Mary's commitment to the suffering Darnley continued to arouse great suspicion in the Scottish court, and a host of unanswerable questions were raised in Edinburgh and elsewhere. Why did Mary bring Darnley back to Edinburgh? What was Bothwell planning?

On the evening of February 10, Mary sat with Darnley at Kirk o' Field. His condition had greatly improved and Darnley was planning to leave for the main castle in the morning. The violet-brown velvet on the bedposts shimmered in the warm firelight as the couple talked. "I have to leave you tonight," Mary said regretfully. "I promised Christiana Hogg and Bastian Pages that I would dance at their wedding masque. I will sleep at Holyrood and see you tomorrow." But Mary left the masque relatively early and spent the evening talking to the earl of Bothwell and John Stewart of Traquair, her guards' captain. She retired rather early to her chambers at Holyrood. A light snow covered the narrow streets, and the chill in the air frosted her palace windows.

As soon as Mary left him, Bothwell changed from his silver carnival doublet to a coarse doublet and black hose. Hiding his face in a riding cloak, Bothwell hurried along the back wall of the south Canongate garden, across the grasses of the crumbling Blackfriars priory, to the east wall of Kirk o' Field, all the while trying to go unnoticed by the Edinburgh night watchmen on patrol.

In the meantime, Darnley was preparing to leave for Holyrood the following day. His two grooms, Glen and MacCraig, packed his valises; Taylor, his valet, encouraged him to play the lute before going to bed.

> *Court life never tamed the primitive woman in her, a woman quick of wit and nimble of body, sensitive, proud, passionate; loyal to her friends, implacable to her enemies; courageous in action, indomitable in purpose.*
> —CONYERS READ
> British historian, on Mary

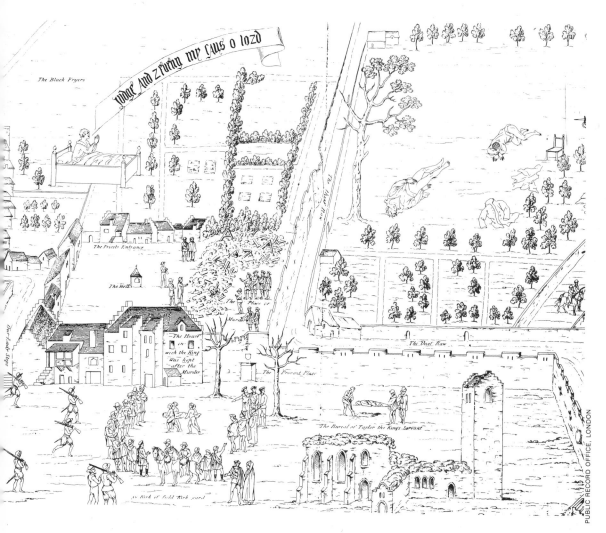

The Black Fryers

mdge And zpung my saus o lozd

The Priests Entrance

The Well

The Place of Murder

The House in wich the King was kept after the Murder

The Provost Place

The Thiel Raw

The Burial of Taylor the Kings Servant

At Kirk of field Kirk yard

Early in the morning of February 11, 1567, the church at Kirk o' Field, where Darnley was convalescing, exploded. This contemporary sketch of the scene shows Darnley (top right, under tree) and a page stripped of their clothes by the blast, but in fact Darnley had been strangled after fleeing from his bedroom.

Outside the night was dark with the new moon. Darnley lay down to sleep.

At 2:00 A.M., the entire town was awakened by a deafening explosion, which echoed through the still winter air. An orange light glowed in the skies above Kirk o' Field. The old church had exploded in fire. The town watchmen ran down the Canongate, and across the Cowgate. In the distance they saw Kirk o' Field in flames.

On the far side of the garden, 70 paces from the building, lay Lord Darnley in a white nightshirt, dead. Bits of red roof tiles, lumber, and dirt from the blast covered his back. But upon closer inspection, no marks from the explosion could be found on his body. The lords who had discovered the body drew back in horror: Darnley had been strangled to death. Next to him lay a dagger, a chair, and a rope — which he had used to escape from his window 14 feet above the alleyway. The grisly scene begged for an explanation.

No one, however, had witnessed the crime, though some nearby peasants did report hearing the victim scream, "Pity me, kinsmen, for the sake of Jesus Christ, who pitied all the world!" But Darnley's cries were muffled by the sound of the explosion. Mary, upon hearing the thunderous blast, ordered messengers to the scene.

It did not take long for suspicion to be voiced. For weeks after the death, masked peasants posted pictures of Bothwell and his friends on the doors and walls of the town, and shrill voices in the night cried forth the names of the accused murderers; Mary received hundreds of desperate pleas. Rumors were whispered in the pubs and markets: "Queen Mary killed the king to wed her lover, Bothwell." Denunciations of Mary were heard: "The whore!" "The murderess!"

On March 1 Mary woke to find perhaps the most powerful evidence of her subjects' disfavor. The walls of Edinburgh were covered with a new, even more scandalous placard: The queen was depicted naked to the waist as a mermaid — the common 16th-century symbol for a prostitute. Beside her Bothwell was illustrated as a hare, the animal of the Hepburn family crest, amid a circle of swords, the weapons of a murderer.

Historians do not know who spread the gunpowder which set Kirk o' Field ablaze, or who tied the rope which strangled the king, but Bothwell was persistently accused of the crime. There is no evidence that Mary actually helped to plan her husband's murder, but her fierce love for Bothwell would appear to implicate her beyond any defense she could offer. Once again Mary had entrusted her counsel to a devious man. Her relationship with Bothwell — already a source of great controversy — would soon prove to be the queen's undoing.

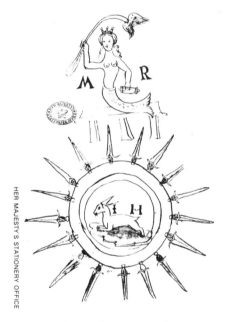

This placard, portraying Mary as a mermaid, the symbol for a prostitute, appeared in the streets of Edinburgh shortly after Darnley's murder. The hare appears on the Bothwell family crest. There were no witnesses to Darnley's death, and the suspicion quickly grew that Bothwell and Mary had conspired to kill the king.

9

A Fatal Embrace

The Privy Council offered a £2,000 reward for the apprehension of Darnley's murderers, but few high-ranking nobles were concerned with the investigation. In fact, they were quite satisfied to be rid of the intolerable king. Mary, widowed for the second time, fell into a state of despair. Moreover, she lacked both the personal strength and trustworthy advisers necessary to placate the public outrage.

Whereas Darnley was considered incompetent as ruler, after the murder his subjects called him an "innocent lamb." Even Elizabeth referred to him as her "slaughtered cousin." Above all, Darnley's father, the earl of Lennox, demanded retribution for his son's death. A trial was finally announced for April 12, 1567; under pressure from Lennox, Parliament would meet in private to try Bothwell as Darnley's murderer.

The Queen, according to the ancient custom should have keeped herself 40 days within, and the doores and windowes should have been closed in token of mourning: but the windowes were opened, to let in light, the fourth day. Before the twelfth day, she went out . . . Bothwell never parting from her side.

—JOHN KNOX
leader of the Scottish Protestants, on Mary's behavior after Darnley's death

---

Mary's association — some called it an infatuation — with Bothwell was disastrous for both of them. In shock and despair, Mary seemed unable to cope with the uproar she faced after Darnley's murder, and Bothwell soon made his bid for complete power.

THE BETTMANN ARCHIVE

On the day the trial was set to begin, 4,000 of Bothwell's supporters swarmed through Edinburgh, a show of force that caused Lennox and his six counselors to stay away from the court. Bothwell was automatically acquitted of complicity in the crime, enabling him to continue his by now unabashedly open quest for power. The earl of Bothwell's star was quickly rising in the Scottish court. Following the trial, he was awarded two strong castles, Dunbar, "the fort upon a point" by the North Sea, and Edinburgh, the citadel of the capital city. Soon a new wave of rumors indicated that Bothwell planned to marry the queen.

On April 19 Bothwell carried out his next carefully planned move. He drew up a document in defense of his own innocence in the Darnley affair and set out his intentions for Mary. He described the young widow as "destitute of a husband, in which solitary state, the commonwealth may not permit her to remain." Bothwell then proposed his own "affection-

Edinburgh Castle, the city's most famous landmark. Bothwell was given the castle after a show trial acquitted him of any guilt in Darnley's murder. The appearance in Edinburgh of thousands of Bothwell's men was intended as a warning to the earl's opponents.

Mary's son, James. The queen could not know that when she visited James, then almost a year old, at Stirling Castle in April 1567, she was seeing her son for the last time. James would be raised by the Protestant Scottish lords, and he later repudiated his mother's Catholic religion.

ate and hearty service . . . and his other good qualities" as evidence for his worthiness as Mary's suitor. Next he invited 28 bishops, earls, and barons to Ainslie's Tavern in Edinburgh for drinking and feasting. At the end of the evening, most of the nobles — by then sufficiently drunk — happily signed the statement, which was later called the "Ainslie Bond." At the bottom of the decree was their promise to support Bothwell's marriage to Mary, be it by counsel, vote, or assistance. Indeed, Bothwell had become so sure of himself that he boasted that he would wed Mary "whether she would herself or not!"

Two days after the bond was signed, Mary arrived at Stirling Castle for a supposedly secret visit with her baby prince. It would be the last time that she ever saw her son. Mary stayed for two days, then gathered her 30 horsemen for the journey back to the capital on April 24, 1567 — exactly nine years after her marriage to Francis II.

Six miles out of Edinburgh, the royal entourage saw 800 armed men across the Bridges of Almond. At their head rode Bothwell, wielding his broadsword and shield. The earl, brimming with confidence, approached Mary, taking her horse by the bridle. Mary's men were helpless in the face of Bothwell's multitudes, and the queen was taken captive. Mary quietly acquiesced, assuring her men that she would rather go with Bothwell than cause needless fighting.

For 40 miles Bothwell rode before the passive queen on the way to Dunbar Castle. Mary sought no help from the concerned peasants witnessing the unusually peaceful abduction. Mary's nobles had been well aware of the earl's scheme, and it appears that Mary and Bothwell were indeed in connivance. Even so, no one, the queen included, seems to have guessed the lengths to which Bothwell would go to assure Mary's agreement to marry him.

Once inside Dunbar Castle, Bothwell completed his plan. In his unending ambition for the throne, he would stop at nothing to wed Mary. Finally alone with the unprotected queen, Bothwell attacked her, believing that the forced union would leave her no choice but to agree to their marriage. As one of

On her return to Edinburgh, Mary is surrounded by Bothwell and his troops in April 1567. In an elaborate scheme to secure his marriage to Mary, Bothwell staged this abduction, to which Mary is thought to have acquiesced. With the subsequent announcement of their wedding, Mary had, in the eyes of most of her subjects, reduced herself to a mere prostitute.

Mary's advisers who had also been taken prisoner explained, "The queen could not but marry him, seeing he had ravished her and lain with her against her will." Although Mary had been quite fond of the scheming Bothwell, the violent attack was of course a demoralizing, shattering experience. She had not foreseen that Bothwell had planned to seal his right to the Scottish crown in so irrevocable a fashion.

Mary felt she could only make legal what was already a consummate union. Mentally and physically weakened from the recent trials of state, Mary had become dangerously lethargic and lacked good judgment. Upon being shown the Ainslie Bond, she automatically assumed that her court supported Bothwell as sovereign. She herself felt she needed a strong and able consort, and Bothwell had proven himself a powerful leader. The only obstacle to be removed was Bothwell's wife, who readily agreed to a divorce. On Thursday, May 15, Mary and Bothwell were wed at Holyrood.

The hasty wedding ceremony, compared to the first lavish celebration in Paris, and even to the second marriage at Holyrood, was perhaps the most difficult event of Mary's young life. In the public eye, Mary was no better than a prostitute.

The small Protestant ceremony, conducted with scant preparation, demonstrated to both Catholic Mary and her court the extent to which her power had fallen into the hands of the earl. She no longer controlled her realm, nor her life. Mary had risked not only her reputation but also the government of Scotland on a marriage to a man who was no more able than Darnley to govern her realm or love her as his wife.

Mary had withstood the shame of the wedding as a last, desperate attempt to bring order to a divided country. She soon realized, however, that the union might very well provoke her political downfall. The jealous nobles were angered by Bothwell's ascension to consort, and they began a conspiracy aimed at parting the royal couple. Moreover, Mary's decision had taken a toll on her emotional stability — more than once Mary threatened suicide to relieve herself of the unending anxieties plaguing her life.

> *By the consenting testimony of the time, the return of their Queen, with all the glamour of youth, beauty, and an interesting personal history, went to the heart of the Scottish people. Skillfully used, the charm of her youth, her sex, her grace and accomplishments, should eventually have assured her the general support of her country. Fortunately for the future of Protestantism, Mary possessed little of the steady prudence and personal dignity of her mother.*
>
> —P. HUME BROWN
> British historian

The rebellious sentiments being heard now were different from those Mary had faced in the past. Revolts such as the run-about-raid, and even Riccio's murder, were justified by the conspirators as being for the public good. Mary's marriage presented the nobles with an opportunity to rally the populace with moral arguments, a much more potent force. Their cry was simple: the queen had wed the murderer of her husband. Soon, the people's outrage knew no bounds, and the nobles gathered their forces.

One noble in particular had cause for revenge — Sir James Balfour, who banded together with the friends of Moray, long-standing enemies of Both-

During the battle of Carberry Hill on June 15, 1567, rebel forces defeated Bothwell's troops and took Mary prisoner. In this sketch Mary is shown (center) being led on horseback to her enemies after surrendering.

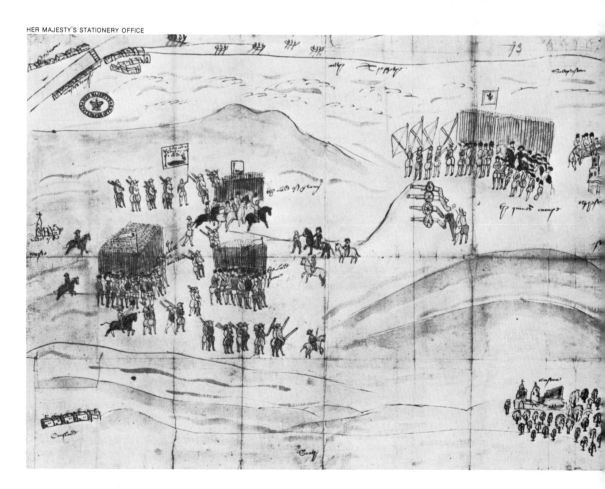

Mary gave her husband a final embrace before surrendering to the rebels at Carberry Hill. It would be the last
time she saw him. Having bartered her liberty for his safe
escape, she would be repaid by his desertion.

well. Balfour's political career had been marked by treachery and a willingness to change sides if personal gain was to be had. A Calvinist, he had been a target of the Riccio murderers, helped plan Darnley's murder, was an adviser to Mary, and had been named captain of Edinburgh Castle. Balfour wanted to regain possession of the castle from Bothwell; the other nobles arrayed alongside him had allegiances of their own, which inspired the conspiracy to bring down the new consort.

On June 6 Balfour attacked the castle of Borthwick, where Mary and Bothwell were staying. Bothwell escaped on horse, leaving Mary alone to defend herself. During the night the queen escaped, disguised as a young man, and rode through the moorlands to meet Bothwell at the Black Castle of Cakemuir. The two then took refuge in Dunbar Castle, with Balfour following closely.

The decisive battle between the royal army and Balfour's troops took place on June 15, 1567, at Carberry Hill near Musselburgh, eight miles east of Edinburgh. Mary's troops, discouraged and badly outnumbered, exchanged only a few desperate volleys with the conspirators. Finally, at sunset, Mary agreed to Bothwell's plan: he would ride back to Dunbar to organize more troops for a grand attack. At the summit of the hill, in view of both armies, Mary and Bothwell held each other in a farewell embrace; Mary promised her fidelity and allegiance. Bothwell departed for the distant castle. Mary would never see her husband again. Bothwell had deserted his army, his new throne, his bride of one month, and his unborn baby — Mary was pregnant with Bothwell's child. (Bothwell was later driven out of Scotland, imprisoned in Denmark for seducing a Norwegian girl and incurring financial debts, and died in prison after going insane.)

Again alone and helpless, Mary surrendered. In exchange for Bothwell's safe passage, Mary had agreed to turn herself in, thinking that with Bothwell gone her opposition would again show allegiance to her. But she had underestimated how discontented with her they had become. She was taken prisoner, never to be released.

> *Wherefore, with regard to the Queen of Scots in particular, it is not his intention to have any further communication with her, unless, indeed, in times to come he shall see some better sign of her life and religion than he has witnessed in the past.*
> —the cardinal of Alessandria, speaking for the pope, from a 1567 letter to the bishop of Mondovi

10

The Ring of Defeat

Mary knew she would never forget that moment atop Carberry Hill. Her first moments as Balfour's prisoner were a marked contrast to the last minute of tenderness she had shared with Bothwell, as the horrible accusations were heaped upon her by the opposing lords: "Burn the whore!" "Kill the murderess!" Dirty and half-naked in a torn petticoat, the prisoner-queen was marched slowly through the capital city. Her angry subjects laughed and hurled insults as she passed; now stripped of all her jewelry and the glory of her reign, Mary hid her face in her hands.

Above the procession flew the flag of the conspirators — a picture of Darnley's corpse and the kneeling Prince James. Above the figures was the baby's cry, "Judge and revenge my cause, O Lord!" The angry Scots were taking their revenge on the 25-year-old queen.

Mary was thrown into a small stone cell in the provost's house opposite Marcat Cross. Shouting townspeople gathered beneath her window. Mary,

Burn her, burn the whore, she is not worthy to live.
—shouts of the crowd that lined the route to Mary's prison

After her capture at Carberry Hill, Mary would spend most of the remainder of her life behind prison walls. Reading, needlework, and writing were her only pastimes; she was allowed little exercise. Yet Mary continued to believe she would somehow regain her freedom and rule Scotland once more.

deserted by her husband, scorned as a whore by her subjects, and held captive by her own government, leaned out to the crowds and shouted, "Good people! Either satisfy your hatred and cruelty by taking my miserable life, or relieve me from the hands of these infamous and inhuman traitors!" Mary's face was black with soot and tears. Was this their regal queen, once so elegant, or a murdering, filthy whore?

For safety the lords moved Mary from Edinburgh to the formidable castle of Lochleven, guarded by the jailer Sir William Douglas. Only four years earlier Mary had sat at Lochleven as a new queen eager to rule both Protestants and Catholics in peace. Mary now returned to the island fortress a devastated prisoner, pregnant, sick, deserted by friends and countrymen. Knox had been right, Mary realized at last: Protestants and Catholics would never tolerate compromise in Scotland. Indeed, the Protestants were close to gaining victory in the once-Catholic land. Mary was suffering the birth pangs of the new religion.

> *I have put in hasard for him both fame and conscience,*
> *I will for his sake renounce the world,*
> *I will die to set him forwart.*
> —from a sonnet, reputedly by Queen Mary, about Bothwell

On the evening of June 16, 1567, Douglas rowed Mary across the 12-mile loch to her prison, where she collapsed from exhaustion into a semi-coma. For days she lay near death, a death welcomed by many of the nobles, who wanted to place Prince James on the throne. They did not want his reign stained by an act of usurpation: Mary must die.

Moreover, the lords had become quite certain of Mary's guilt in Darnley's murder. Two days after her arrival in prison, the lords received a small silver casket covered with green velvet. Inside they found letters and sonnets from Mary to Bothwell, written before Darnley's death. If the letters were authentic, they unquestionably linked Mary to the crime. Her words proclaimed that she was indeed in love with Bothwell, that she hoped to marry him, and that she was wooing her husband to win his confidence — and then lead him to his death, with Bothwell's help. These "Casket Letters" are believed by most historians to be in Mary's own hand, although their authenticity is still debated.

If the lords could not kill the murderous queen,

which would provoke the wrath of both England and France, they could force her voluntary abdication. Taking advantage of her weakened condition — Mary had also miscarried during the week of July 18, probably from the stress of captivity — Robert Melville and Patrick Lindsay forced Mary to sign the papers of abdication. On July 24, 1567, Mary legally forfeited the crown which had given her "long, great, and intolerable pains." Her baby son would take her place.

On July 29 Mary heard distant drumrolls and church bells ringing: her son had been crowned King James VI. John Knox preached at the coronation, his Protestant followers widely supporting the deposition of the wicked Catholic sovereign. Mary, who had claimed the Scottish throne when she was only seven days old, had actually ruled for just six years. By the age of 25 she had been queen of two countries, wife of three men, and the victor of many battles. And though it looked to opponents and supporters alike that Mary had been defeated once and for all, she herself knew that this was just another trial to be overcome — she would not accept defeat.

Mary was held prisoner at Lochleven for 11 months, joined only by her childhood friend, Mary Seaton, and two maids. Her half brother Moray had

"The Triumph of Faith," from a painting by Titian, the 16th-century Venetian master. Mary's inability to judge a man's character served her badly, to be sure, but the queen also had the misfortune to be the ruler at a time of momentous religious upheaval in England and Scotland — a force that was decidedly beyond her control.

assumed the regency of Scotland until James came of age. Moray kept a close watch on Mary, who spent most of her time embroidering and plotting her escape. Mary's small tower looked out over the western loch near Kinross; she wondered how many suns would set before she gained her freedom.

Mary still had close allies in the Scottish Hamiltons, who had long been archenemies of Moray. Together with the young George Douglas, a 16-year-old page in Lochleven, they devised a plan to rescue Mary from captivity. George had become infatuated with the beautiful prisoner; by complaining of his "rude advances," Mary was able to send him ashore to join the Hamiltons and arrange for her escape.

On the evening of May 2, 1568, Mary received word that all was ready. Willy Douglas — one of George's cousins — stole the keys to the prison door and was waiting at a small boat on the loch landing. Mary, disguised as a page, slipped down the dark passages and out to the water's edge.

The vessel, with Mary hidden under the seat, arrived on the opposite shore to meet George and 200 horsemen, who accompanied the fugitives to a castle in Linlithgowshire, near Hamilton Palace. Hundreds of earls, bishops, and barons had taken an oath to return Mary to her rightful throne. Soon Mary had an army of 6,000 men. The queen loudly retracted her abdication and, with her hair streaming down her back and a confident army behind her, set out to overtake the troops of Moray.

Eleven days later, however, Mary's army suffered a devastating defeat. In less than an hour, hundreds of Hamilton's men were slaughtered by Moray's forces in the Battle of Langside, the fight that was to decide Mary's fate. Mary, watching the painful sight of her kingdom being taken by force, was again faced with a crucial decision: where could she seek asylum? In England or France? "I shall never return to France as a fugitive!" Mary proclaimed defiantly. "Never to a country where I have worn the Crown-Matrimonial!"

Mary suddenly knew her only recourse: she must take refuge in England. Elizabeth was of her own flesh and blood. She had sent Mary her royal ring

In July 1567 Mary, imprisoned at Lochleven, was forced to sign her abdication of the Scottish throne. Her infant son would take her place, just as she had been crowned while still a child. Mary's half brother Moray, who had always coveted her throne, was now in power as regent to young James VI.

Mary's maid and page kneel before their captive queen. Behind her stands Mary Seaton, a loyal friend ever since they had embarked together for France years earlier. Mary Seaton would remain with her queen through her long imprisonment.

as a token of loyalty while Mary was in Lochleven. Surely, she thought, she could trust her cousin. Mary wrote to Elizabeth: "By unexpected means, the Almighty Disposer of all things delivered me from the cruel imprisonment I underwent; but I have since lost a battle in which most of those who preserved their loyal integrity fell before my eyes."

"I am now forced out of my kingdom, and driven to such straits that, next to God, I have no hope but in your goodness!"

"I beseech you, therefore, my dearest sister, that I may be conducted in your presence, that I may acquaint you with all my affairs. In the meantime, I beseech God to grant you all heavenly benedictions, and to me patience and consolation, which last I hope and pray to obtain by your means."

Mary took the jeweled ring off her finger and slipped it between the pages of the letter: "To remind you of the reasons I have to depend on England, I send back to its Queen this token, the jewel of her promised friendship and assistance. Your affectionate sister, M.R."

But the sparkling ring had blinded Mary to the true character of her cousin. Elizabeth had not forgotten how desperately Mary had pursued her throne. Suddenly, she was in a position to guarantee that Mary would never take her crown nor regain the crown of the Scottish kingdom.

11

Castles in the Air

Mary rode 60 miles in one day after the Battle of Langside, accompanied by six lords. The small party arrived on the shores of the Solway Firth the following afternoon and boarded a ship for England, hoping to secure protection for the fugitive queen. But as they left the mists of the Lowlands behind, Mary suddenly changed her mind. Perhaps having a premonition of the dire fate that awaited her in England, Mary decided she must go to France instead. However, the summer winds were strong that day, as strong as they had been when she sailed from France to Scotland as a widowed queen. The gale decided her fate: Mary set sail for England, never to see her native Scotland again.

Indeed, it was as though Elizabeth were navigating the vessel. Were the deposed Mary to take refuge in France, Elizabeth reasoned, Mary might challenge the English throne with an even greater fervor. Furthermore, Elizabeth knew that she could not allow her cousin to return to Scotland — the Protestant and Catholic battles were only exacerbated by the presence of a Catholic sovereign, regardless of her claim to the throne.

Remember that the theatre of the world is wider than the realm of England.
—MARY, QUEEN OF SCOTS
to her judges, October 1586

Mary gazes sadly to the skies, hoping for a miraculous escape from her English confinement. After her escape and the subsequent defeat of her army by Moray at Langside, Mary had felt her only recourse was to flee to her cousin Elizabeth and seek sanctuary in England. The English queen, however, was determined to prevent Mary from ever coming to power.

A tapestry with a unicorn motif, woven by Mary while she was in prison in England. Unicorns represented the arms of Scotland, which Mary was never to see again. Part fantasy, part autobiography, Mary's tapestries often reflected her innermost thoughts. They also protected her against the cold and dampness of her surroundings.

94

Upon her arrival in England, Mary was taken captive. Indeed, for most of the year she remained a closely watched prisoner. She pleaded with Elizabeth to grant her an audience, and begged to be released from the drafty castles in which the English sovereign kept her. But Elizabeth would not forgive Mary for marrying Bothwell and for her suspected involvement in Darnley's murder, and decided not to grant her cousin the dignity of a royal audience until Mary's name had been cleared.

Mary continued to plead her cause through various ministers and councilors, but to no avail. Finally, during the winter, the queen granted Mary a full investigation of the murder. The York-Westminster conference lasted from October 1568 to January 1569, during which the Casket Letters were examined for authenticity. Mary offered no defense, thinking it beneath her to justify her behavior against people she saw as treasonous rebels. Moray, in England to present his case, condemned his half sister as fully and solely responsible for Darnley's death, saying that Bothwell had only followed the orders of the murderous queen. Elizabeth closed the proceedings after Mary had been sufficiently discredited but without proclaiming the guilt either of Mary for murder or of Moray for treason. Though her prospects for any political redemption or resurgence appeared dim at this point, Mary was still considered too "dangerous" to be set free. Her "appetite" for the Scottish and English thrones had by no means abated.

Her Scottish hopes were dealt another blow in January 1570 with the murder of Moray by James Hamilton; Lennox, Darnley's father, assumed the regency of Scotland the following July. Mary's last few Scottish supporters were defeated, and with them her hopes of being rescued and returned to her homeland were now virtually nonexistent.

Mary's unending incarceration began. The days were almost interminable for the helpless queen. Slowly the vibrant, beautiful young woman became an embittered, rheumatic prisoner. Her tall frame gradually bowed from ceaseless hours of letter writing and embroidery; her long auburn hair was

Mary remained the great "untouchable" in English politics—rebellious, defiant, incorrigible in her hope of ultimate victory.
—J.B. BLACK
British historian

Mary setting sail from Solway Firth in 1568 to seek refuge in England. Instinctively, she tried at the last minute to make for France instead of England, but ill winds prevailed. Mary was taken captive as soon as she landed in England, and her pleas for an audience with Elizabeth remained unanswered.

sheared by her captors to accommodate the medicines applied for her frequent headaches; her arms and legs grew twisted and atrophied from arthritis.

Elizabeth allowed Mary only the smallest court for companionship and nursing. Her closest lady-in-waiting, Mary Seaton, stayed with the queen until she herself was too old to tolerate the damp and sunless cell. Once a great lover of the outdoors, Mary was allowed only sporadically to venture beyond her prison walls. On those few occasions, hardly able to walk without support, Mary was carried in a chair to watch the nobles duck-hunting in a nearby pond.

Mary occupied herself almost ceaselessly with her needle and thread. Tapestries depicting gold and silver unicorns, apple trees, pomegranates, crowns, and crosses covered the walls of her cell; she created an embroidered kingdom of ships and castles to rule. Indeed, the many political and personal webs she had woven during her reign seemed to come alive again in the designs of her threads. In many ways, Mary had never given up her kingdom; she would continue to see herself as queen until her death. On one large tapestry Mary embroidered a crowned phoenix rising from a fire. Above it she inscribed, "En ma fin est mon commencement" — "In my end is my beginning," the motto of her mother.

High up in many castle towers, Mary was held prisoner for 19 years. From her prison at Tutbury Castle, Mary wrote: "To convey to you an idea of my present situation, I am on all sides enclosed by fortified walls on the summit of a hill, which lies exposed to every wind of heaven. . . . I leave you to judge in what manner such humidity must act on the human body, and to say everything in a word, the apartments are in general more like dungeons prepared for the vilest criminals than a habitation suited to a person of my quality."

"I have for my own person two little miserable chambers, so intensely cold during the night that, but for ramparts and entrenchments of tapestry and curtains, it would be impossible to prolong my existence. . . ."

"The only light admitted is from an aperture nine feet in circumference. For taking air and exercise, either on foot or in my chair, I have but about a quarter of an acre behind the stables."

Mary was not, however, completely isolated as a prisoner. She was allowed a certain amount of correspondence, through which she could remain in contact with her English backers. She also posed

Tutbury Castle, one of the places where Mary was imprisoned. Her 19 years as a captive were marked by involvement—through the correspondence she was permitted — with conspiracies aimed at ending Queen Elizabeth's reign. Even in prison Mary remained a powerful symbol for Catholics in Scotland and England.

Mary's son is crowned in 1603 as James I, king of England. In 1584 he had repudiated his mother and allied himself with the Protestants. Mary, who would not live to see James rule either Scotland (as King James VI) or England, laid a curse upon her son.

something of a problem for Elizabeth. Her being alive at all, even if she was discredited and disgraced and had only small pockets of support, meant she was still an inspiration to any plotters — especially Catholics — still seeking Elizabeth's ouster. Elizabeth did not seem to want to execute her cousin, at least not yet. Thus, Mary became the focus of several plots aimed at ending Elizabeth's rule and installing Mary as queen of England.

The first, in 1569, involved an uprising of the earls of Northumberland and Westmorland. They wanted Mary to marry the duke of Norfolk and then reinstate a Catholic regime in England. When this revolt was put down, Norfolk conspired with Robert Rodolfi, an Italian banker based in London. In 1572 they planned to murder Elizabeth and bring over the Spanish army from the Netherlands to back their bid for power. However, the plot — which Mary knew of — was discovered and the duke was put to death. The English Parliament demanded Mary's execution as well, but Elizabeth refused to sanction such a move. She did, however, make public all the evidence regarding Mary's involvement in Darnley's murder, another severe blow to Mary's public standing. Another plot, this one put into motion by the duke of Guise in 1583, called for an association between Mary and her son to rule Scotland. But in 1584 James VI repudiated the plan, not wanting his mother to interfere with his claim to the throne. The young James threw himself in with the Protestants, and fully denounced his mother as a murderess and whore. When Mary heard of her son's disloyalty and entry into an independent alliance with Elizabeth, she felt that she had lost all hope of ever reclaiming her honor. Even her son had betrayed her.

"A mother's curse shall light upon him!" she wrote. "I will deprive him of all the greatness to which through me he can pretend. He shall have nothing but what he inherits from his father!" Mary refused to relinquish her dreams of sovereignty. "Without him I am, and shall be of right, as long as I live, his queen and sovereign, but he independently of me, can only be Lord Darnley or earl of Lennox." But the only kingdom Mary could rule was the small kingdom of her silk imaginings. James VI had already been crowned in the parish church of Stirling. In June 1587, at the age of 17, he would legally assume the right to govern Scotland — now officially Protestant.

But Mary would not live to see her son take the throne: Elizabeth had other plans. The English sovereign had come to realize that only Mary's death could prevent powerful Catholic factions in England from rescuing her and promoting a new Catholic queen. As the general outcry against Mary grew more violent, Mary faced one last battle in the unending war between Catholics and Protestants. The woman whose reign had ushered in a new Scottish religion was about to become its terrible victim.

> *I beg you to obtain for me some turtle-doves and Barbary fowls, that I may try to bring them up in this country. I should take pleasure in feeding them in their cages, as I do all the little birds I can find. These are the only pastimes of a prisoner.*
> —MARY, QUEEN OF SCOTS
> from a letter to the Scottish ambassador to France

12

The Flight of the Phoenix

Mary's fortunes seemed to take a turn for the better. A supporter named Gifford offered his services in secret to deliver and receive Mary's correspondence. Little did Mary know that every letter was being carefully studied by English guards for any clues of treason or escape plans. Elizabeth had embarked on an effort to gather the evidence necessary to try Mary for treason.

One sunny summer day Mary was graciously invited to a stag hunt given by a neighboring noble. Mary, though stiff from her confinement, was still capable of riding, and eagerly accepted his welcome. As the hunting horns sounded and the horses were released, it soon became apparent that Mary herself was the target of the day's sport. Her horse was led away from the grounds and Mary, perplexed as to where she was being taken, dropped to her knees and refused to go any farther.

Suddenly, she understood the plan. While she was away from her chambers the queen's party was searching her private papers back in her cell. They would find her letters — particularly those from Anthony Babington, an English conspirator who had planned to invade England with 100 men, join

She has had her revenge, if not on Elizabeth living, yet on her memory in the annals of her country.
—J.A. FROUDE
British historian, on Mary

Mary's death warrant is read to her after she was pronounced guilty of treason in 1587. Although Queen Elizabeth had wished to avoid executing Mary, the Scottish queen's constant schemes for escape, which she foolishly committed to paper, finally sealed her fate.

AETATIS SVÆ 68

Sir Francis Walsingham, the captain of Elizabeth's guards. He had slyly planted spies to intercept Mary's prison letters and then decoyed her away from her chambers so that the incriminating letters could be confiscated and used as evidence against her.

forces with other Catholic supporters, rescue Mary, and then kill Elizabeth. Evidence of such a plot was all Elizabeth needed to prosecute her cousin.

The English government savagely executed the Babington conspirators: "They were all cut down, their privities were cut off, bowelled alive and seeing, and quartered." Mary suspected that her own death was now imminent, although she did not believe the accusations of "treason." Instead, Mary saw herself as a formidable challenger to the throne and as a Catholic martyr in a Protestant land. She would be tried before a jury of Protestant counselors. Surely they could invent ample cause to execute a Catholic.

On September 25, 1586, Mary was imprisoned in the dungeon tower of Fotheringhay Castle. Her trial began on October 15 in the castle's great hall. At 9:00 A.M. on that day, Mary quietly put away her needle and thread, smoothed her black velvet gown, and readied herself to face her destiny. She prepared herself for the inevitable sentence of death.

Mary's French physician and Scottish attendant escorted her down the staircase to the long hall below. Her faded black train moved slowly across the floor with her faltering steps. She approached the upper end of the room where an empty throne was placed next to a small prisoner's chair. As Mary saw the multitudes before her, she sadly remarked, "Ah! Here are many counselors, but not one for me!" Mary started to take her place on the empty throne, but was halted by the hand of a lord. She hesitated for a moment, and sadly cried to the expressionless jury, "I am a queen by right of birth! My place is on the throne!" The lords, however, scorned her as a whore and murderess. Mary took her place in the prisoner's chair, where she desperately battled to save her life.

The trial came to order. Mary wholly denied her involvement in the conspiracy. "I cannot walk without assistance nor use my arms!" she pleaded. "I spend most of my time confined to bed by sickness." Was this a conspirator against the powerful English sovereign? she asked. "My advancing age and bodily weakness both prevent me from wishing to resume the reins of government. I have perhaps only two or three years to live in this world, and I do not aspire to any public position, especially when I consider the pain and desperance which meet those who wish to do right, and act with justice and dignity in the midst of so perverse a generation, and when a whole world is full of crimes and troubles!"

These were the final, desperate words of a condemned woman. It was apparent to all convened that Elizabeth had crushed the vital spirit of the passionate Mary, queen of the Scots. The English

As a sinner I am truly conscious of having often offended my Creator and I beg him to forgive me, but as a Queen and Sovereign, I am aware of no fault or offence for which I have to render account.
—MARY, QUEEN OF SCOTS
October 1586

THE BETTMANN ARCHIVE

Mary being led to her execution. The courage and passion she showed in the face of her death was testimony to her personal strength. Adhering to her faith to the end, she even refused the prayers of a Protestant minister.

queen, whose primary concern was the safeguarding of her own power, could not allow Mary to continue to be the focus of Catholic rebellion in England. For the protection of her Protestant realm, Elizabeth agreed to sign the order condemning Mary to death.

On February 8, 1587, Mary prepared for her execution. The black velvet draping her bed indicated that she already felt herself to be a dead woman. As her maids knelt to pray for her, the sheriff knocked on her prison door. "Madam, the lords have sent me for you." Mary lifted her face, which was as pale as the moon she had gazed upon for so many years from her high citadels. She looked one last time at the kingdom of tapestries surrounding her — the wild birds, the golden unicorns, the great crowned phoenix rising from the flames. How many troubles she had survived! Her first husband died as a new king, her second was murdered as a weak and worthless consort, her third had gone insane in prison. Her son had disowned her. There was nothing left of her power as queen. The sheriff was waiting at the door. "Yes," she said softly, "let us go."

In the middle of the great hall a large stage, draped in black, supported a small black block and a shining axe. Beside them stood a stool for Mary.

Mary slowly mounted the steps of the stage. Her execution command was pronounced loudly to the surrounding spectators. A Protestant minister offered to pray for her. "I am settled in the ancient Catholic Roman religion, and mind to spend my blood in defense of it!" Mary protested. She prayed aloud for England, asking forgiveness for the executioner who held the axe.

"I forgive you with all my heart, for now I hope you shall make an end of all my troubles."

During the last moments in her cell Mary had written a prayer in her "Book of Devotion," and she

A contemporary Dutch watercolor depicts the beheading of Mary on February 8, 1587. It was a cold winter morning, but a large crowd had gathered to witness Mary's final hour. The queen was led to the center of the hall, where, disrobed and blindfolded, she calmly submitted to the axe. Before she died she offered a prayer for the welfare of England and its queen.

quietly recited this psalm as her maids helped remove her dress and bind her eyes with a white embroidered cloth:

> O Lord my God, I have trusted in thee;
> O Jesu my dearest one, now set me free.
> In prison's oppression, in sorrow's obsession,
> I weary for thee.
> With sighing and crying bowed down as dying,
> I adore thee, I implore thee, set me free!

Mary was left standing in her red petticoat and sleeves. To some, the red was the color of a Catholic martyr; to others it boldly illustrated her whoring and murderous ways.

Mary knelt and placed her head on the block, turning her heavy gold crucifix to her back. The axe was poised over her neck. She closed her eyes and whispered, "*In manus tuas, Domine, confide spiritum meum.*" ("Into your hands, O Lord, I commend my spirit.") Elizabeth's order was then fulfilled: Mary, queen of Scots, was beheaded. The phoenix had flown from the fire; Mary had found her peace.

The hawk of England had circled Mary from her

Bust of Mary, queen of Scots. A century after her son became King James I of England (the first of four Stuart kings), the two hostile countries of Scotland and England were officially combined to form the united nation of Great Britain.

THE BETTMANN ARCHIVE

birth to her death, from the events following the Battle of Solway Moss to the English court at Fotheringhay Castle. Mary's reign was one of constant trouble and heartache, as she struggled to guard her Catholic crown from the English, the French, and the Protestants in her own kingdom. Had she heeded John Knox's advice, perhaps Mary's passions would not have resulted in the execution block. Compromise was not possible in Scotland. The unification that Mary so desperately wanted with England could only be possible under a Protestant sovereign, who turned out to be her son James VI. Indeed, in 1603 James Stuart became James I, king of England; though the official union of the two countries would not occur for another 100 years, his rule made that day much more likely.

Mary Stuart remains one of the most mysterious queens in history. Was she a martyr for her faith and country, or was she responsible for murder, adultery, and deceit? In the end, we are left only with her colorful tapestries, her melancholy letters and poems, and the sad drama of a vital young woman who, from the beginning, allowed her passions to rule her ever-divided kingdom. Mary died as she was born, caught in the religious battle between Catholics and Protestants. Indeed, perhaps in her very beginning was the end of Mary Stuart, queen of the Scots.

Further Reading

Ashton, Robert. *Reformation and Revolution 1558–1660*. New York: Oxford University Press, 1984.

Byrd, Elizabeth. *Maid of Honour: The Court of Mary Queen of Scots*. London: Macmillan, 1978.

Cowan, Ian B. *The Enigma of Mary Stuart*. New York: St. Martin's Press, 1971.

Donaldson, Gordon. *Mary Queen of Scots*. London: English Universities Press, 1974.

———. *All the Queen's Men: Power and Politics in Mary Stewart's Scotland*. New York: St. Martin's Press, 1983.

Fallon, Frederic. *The White Queen*. Garden City, N.Y.: Doubleday, 1972.

Hibbert, Eleanor. *Mary Queen of Scots: The Fair Devil of Scotland*. New York: Putnam, 1975.

Plowden, Alison. *Two Queens in One Isle: The Deadly Relationship of Elizabeth I and Mary Queen of Scots*. Brighton: Harvester Press, 1984.

Chronology

Dec. 8, 1542	Born Mary Stuart; a week later, Mary inherits the crown when her father, King James V of Scotland, dies
1543	The Treaties of Greenwich, guaranteeing Mary's marriage to the British crown prince, ratified, then broken
1544–45	England invades Scotland
1547	English occupation of southeast Scotland
1548	Mary sent to France to ensure her safety
April 24, 1558	Marries Francis, crown prince of France
July 1559	Francis II ascends the throne; Mary becomes queen of France
June 1560	Death of Mary's mother, Marie de Guise
July 1560	Mary refuses to ratify the Treaty of Edinburgh, which acknowledges Elizabeth's right to the English throne
Aug. 1560	Protestants win the War of the Reformation in Scotland
Dec. 5, 1560	Death of Mary's husband, King Francis II
Aug. 1561	Mary returns to Scotland
1562	Mary's troops put down rebellion by the earl of Huntly
July 29, 1565	Mary marries Henry Stuart, Lord Darnley
Sept. 1565	The "run-about-raid," instigated by Mary's half brother James Stuart, the earl of Moray, suppressed
March 9, 1566	Murder of Mary's favorite court musician and companion, David Riccio
June 19, 1566	Mary gives birth to Prince James
Feb. 11, 1567	Murder of Darnley
May 15, 1567	Mary marries James Hepburn, the earl of Bothwell
June 15, 1567	Defeated at Carberry Hill and imprisoned
July 1567	Abdicates; her son is crowned King James VI
May 1568	Defeated at the Battle of Langside and flees to England; Queen Elizabeth has Mary imprisoned
Jan. 1569	The York-Westminster conference, investigating Mary's involvement in Darnley's murder, ends inconclusively
1586	Babington plot, involving the invasion of England by Mary's Catholic supporters, revealed
Feb. 8, 1587	Execution of Mary for treason

Index

Sally Stepanek, a graduate of Yale University, is a free-lance writer and editor living in New York. She is also the author of *Martin Luther* and *John Calvin* in the Chelsea House series WORLD LEADERS PAST & PRESENT.

Arthur M. Schlesinger, jr., taught history at Harvard for many years and is currently Albert Schweitzer Professor of the Humanities at City University of New York. He is the author of numerous highly praised works in American history and has twice been awarded the Pulitzer Prize. He served in the White House as special assistant to Presidents Kennedy and Johnson.